SWEDEN

Barry Turner

SWEDEN

B. T. Batsford Ltd
London

First published 1976
© Barry Turner 1976

ISBN ~~0 7134 3158 2~~ 0713431725

Made and printed in Great Britain by
Biddles of Guildford, Surrey.
for the publishers B. T. Batsford Ltd
4 Fitzhardinge Street, London W1
Computer typeset by
Input Typesetting Ltd, London

Contents

The Illustrations

Acknowledgements

The Author and Publishers wish to thank the following for the photographs appearing in this book: Gladys Nicol for plates 7 and 15; Royal Swedish Embassy, London (Press and Information Department, and Tourist Secretary) for plates 2 and 9; Swedish Information for plate 12; Swedish National Tourist Office for plate 14; Swedish National Travel Association, London for plate 6; Swedish Tourist Traffic Association, Stockholm for plates 1,3, 5, 8, 10, 11, 13, and 16; Sten Vilson for plate 4.

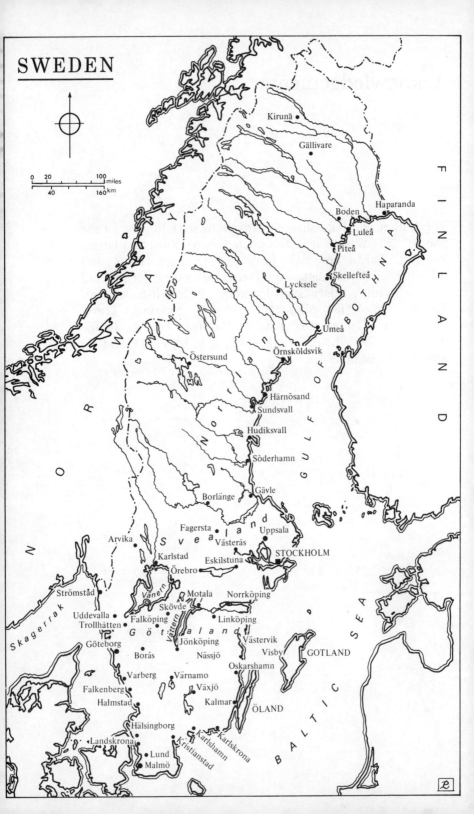

1. Swedes at Home

I came out of Arlanda airport and made for the city bus half closing my eyes against the sharp dawn sunlight of a Swedish summer. There were few other arrivals but the rattle of luggage trolleys on the forecourt was conspicuously loud. The morning rush of travellers was still two hours away and the night staff emerged only briefly to welcome the occasional charter flight. In the otherwise silent concrete jungle of the airport complex there was just one centre of frantic activity. Across the road in the empty bays of the car park two men in white hospital coats manoeuvred a gigantic mobile vacuum between the meters. With brushes whizzing and air tubes sucking the machine lumbered across the tarmac in hungry pursuit of every scrap of litter and every particle of dust. I spoke to a Stockholmer who was sitting next to me in the coach. 'Apparently you like to keep the place clean.' He nodded seriously. 'Not only clean,' he said, 'but healthy.'

My Swedish friends will not easily forgive me for introducing their country with a reference to their innate passion for hygiene. Not that they are in any way ashamed of their preoccupation; it is simply that first-time visitors are liable to associate an excessive regard for cleanliness and order with a certain dullness of spirit and an over-attention to petty detail. The truth is quite otherwise but it is worth stating immediately that Sweden is a neat, clean and well-ordered country which has its strongest appeal for people who appreciate competence and smooth efficiency. Basing all else on this understanding I can go on to reveal that the Swedes are by no means passive and unemotional – least of all when they are debating their philosophy of life and extolling the merits of their homeland. Listen to the true southerner describing the wheat plains of Skåne, a grand sweep of yellow specked with small isolated farm houses and churches. The Stockholmer will tell you proudly that his is one of the most beautiful cities in the world, administered and designed for twentieth-century man but in a way that has avoided the cruder and more disruptive effects of the technological society. The Swede with a strong sense of history inevitably feels a pull towards Dalarna, 'the Heart of Sweden', where the folk traditions of the country are most strongly in evidence. But the claims to distinction of the southerner, the centre and the city dweller are furiously disputed by the people of the north. Over vast areas of this territory nature is allowed to rule – and not simply in the forests where man can at least claim a significant contribution to the continuing expansion in timber production – but in the mountains and lake-filled valleys where the landscape is barely disturbed by occasional habitation and the incursions of the leisure seekers.

Yet however strongly the regions declare their individualism it is the characteristics binding them together that are immediately apparent to the visitor. Sweden is a country of forest, which covers over half the land surface; of water contained in 96,000 lakes and washing 1,000 miles of jigsaw coastline; and of rocks which come in every size and are part of almost every view. Except when the snow falls, which can be anything from one or two months in the south to five months or more in the north, the prevailing colours are green, dark blue, grey and red – the last because so many wooden buildings are painted with iron oxide to preserve the timber. If the combination of colours produces an image of heaviness, dispel the thought. The seasonal shadings of trees, water and rocks create some of the most compelling scenes which are undeniably subdued but never tedious.

And what of the Swedish people? They number about eight million – the same total as the population of London – but they occupy an area of 170,000 square miles. Sweden is the fourth largest country in Europe and is nearly twice the size of the United Kingdom. The great majority of citizens are concentrated in the towns and cities of the south. It is sometimes easy to believe that the north is reserved exclusively for the Lapps, the lumbermen and the tourists. The region of Norrland which covers more than half the area of Sweden provides for less than one-tenth of the population.

But urbanisation is a recent development and while most Swedes appreciate the facilities and opportunities of living in tightly grouped communities, they still have a longing for the countryside. The best evidence for this assertion is the rapidly increasing proportion of families who own holiday and weekend cottages. At present the figure is something like twenty-five per cent and may well reach fifty per cent before the end of the decade. These timbered chalets are seldom luxurious, at least by Swedish standards, but their setting is invariably idyllic. There is space enough in the country for everyone to choose a spot that is essentially their own – on a lake shore, a coastal island, or in a wooded enclave – where they can be free from the pressure of keeping up standards or even bothering to acknowledge the existence of their fellow citizens who, if they have any sense, are miles away enjoying their own share of rural seclusion.

The need for a periodic emotional release of a change of place and mood is probably more important to the Swedes than to other Europeans because the routine of their ordinary daily lives is so tightly and formally administered. Indeed, the Swedes are, by nature, a most correct people, particularly in business matters but also on social occasions. They like to be sure they are saying the right thing at the right time which accounts for their excessive shyness in the early stage of a party before the flow of drinks has drowned that part of their conscience which insists on worrying about what the other person is doing. Then they talk about anything and everything with an intense enthusiasm and frankness that is quite breath-taking. Family and other personal matters which the Anglo-Saxon would keep to himself under pain of torture, are for the Swedish partygoer, an undying source of conversation. Jobs going wrong, marriages breaking up, salaries rising or falling (a Swede will, without a trace of self-consciousness tell you precisely what he earns and will expect you to respond with corresponding frankness) – all these topics are carefully analysed and not in a scandal-mongering way but openly, with the people most closely involved in any particular problem enthusiastically participating in the debate.

An invitation to dinner in a traditional Swedish home can be the preliminary to a formidable evening if no account is taken of the guests' responsibilities. These include bringing a gift of flowers for the hostess and, in the case of the guest of honour who sits to the immediate left of the hostess, giving a speech of thanks. The timing of this address which need not consist of more than a few kindly references to the quality of the food and the charm of the company, is a matter of fine calculation. It is no use waiting for the coffee because the meal can end quite abruptly and if everyone is leaving the table the opportunity of saying anything except 'I'm sorry' is lost forever. The best answer is to take one's cue from the host who will make a short speech of welcome about midway through the first course. A follow-up after the main dish never comes amiss and as a bonus, cuts short speculation as to whether you have done your homework. It should be said that young people are leaning away from the more elaborately structured codes of behaviour but nonetheless the business of eating and drinking can be taken quite seriously by sections of all age groups. For instance, to salute your companion with a friendly 'Skål'! as you raise your glass may be perfectly acceptable in an easy-going party atmosphere but at a formal dinner it is still the general rule to choose a particular recipient for your good wishes and to look directly into the eyes of that person as a 'Skål' is exchanged.

No meal is complete unless the table and other items of furniture are decorated with candles. It seems, in some mysterious way, as if the contentment and happiness of the company relate directly to the number of flickering lights in the room. Indeed, there are moments when I entertain the suspicion that deep down in their national subconscious the Swedes are frustrated pyromaniacs. In rural areas it is quite common for householders to illuminate the evening with naked lights in the gardens or just outside their front doors. And remember these are wooden houses, as often as not surrounded by trees. Candles are especially favoured as a token of celebration. At Christmas many of the churches put on quite a show for their congregation with avenues of tiny flames stretching out a welcome. Compared, say, with a British Guy Fawkes night any of the various Swedish festivals must involve an immense risk of conflagration. Yet, by some miracle, the fire services are not overstretched.

The Swedes do everything earlier than other Europeans. In the summer months, offices are busy at eight in the morning. If you are in a city centre and happen to notice a rush of young people at about 11.30 it is more than likely that the secretaries are on their way to lunch. Don't try ringing any business after four o'clock because everyone will have gone home. And on Friday squeeze all appointments in before three – just to be on the safe side. If a precise time is on an invitation it is meant to be interpreted – precisely. With the sole exception of my wife the Swedes make a great virtue of punctuality. On one of those occasions it would be nice but impossible to forget we gave a party in London for some visiting Swedish teachers, inviting them for seven. At about half past six we darted out for a few last-minute purchases, found, inevitably, that we were held up in the traffic and returned at two minutes to seven, to make embarrassed apologies to forty Swedish guests waiting patiently on the doorstep.

One welcome relaxation in Swedish manners is the decline in the use of titles. There was a time when everyone – but everyone – claimed a title even if it was no more than the label of one's profession. Until recently even the telephone directories were arranged accordingly so that it was impossible to look up, say, Mr Andersson unless you happened to know that he was a plumber in which case you would find him listed as Plumber Andersson. In the old days people went to extraordinary lengths to secure for themselves a signature of distinction. I remember reading somewhere of a visitor to Sweden who discovered in a country churchyard a tombstone which recorded the passing of 'Owner of his own home – Svensson'. Ejoying the story, without taking it very seriously, I retailed the joke to Swedish friends who turned it back on me by revealing that there are parts of the country where the title is still used and treated with respect. But they added the pertinent detail that Swedes are not inclined to string out their names with academic qualifications and awards for loyal service.

The traditional formality of the Swedes relates directly to their sense of social discipline which, in turn, accounts for the fact that the country is so well organised, or, as some would say, over-organised. Everyone accepts that laws and rules are there to be obeyed even if, occasionally, the meaning behind them is not immediately self-evident. One of the more breath-taking experiences for a bloody-minded Anglo-Saxon who instinctively defies such instructions as 'Keep off the Grass' or 'Stand to the Right' is to observe a crowd of pedestrians wanting to cross an entirely clear road yet not daring to move because the red light is against them. But the respect for conformity, at least in matters that might properly be regarded as of public interest, creates advantages that are quickly noticed and appreciated by visitors. For example, the response to the anti-litter campaign has been such that almost any citizen would now feel positively ashamed if he neglected his environmental duties. Michael Frayn writing in *The Observer*, neatly illustrates the point, with his observation of a young drunk on Stockholm Central Station 'struggling halfway up the platform, against some powerful magnetic field which seemed to be trying to divert him from his goal, in order to dutifully deposit an empty cigarette packet in a rubbish-bin'. The idea that an element of fastidiousness is part of the hereditary make-up of every Swede is confirmed by another story, from another journalist, this time published in

The Spectator. The scene is a bookshop in Stockholm. 'A baby girl, not more than three, strapped in her push-chair, accidentally brushes against a book. It falls to the floor. Leaning down, straining against her straps, she picks it up with great effort and puts it back on the pile. It isn't quite straight. Leaning right out of her push chair she realigns it with the books underneath, and sinks back with a sigh'.

There are those who say that the neat and orderly society approaches too closely to a benevolent dictatorship. To support this claim the critic's first line of evidence is the Identity Card, a small wallet-sized document containing a photograph and the basic life details of the holder. Just about every Swedish citizen carries an identity card, the number of which links him with the computer network of the central administration and the social services. The very idea of being reduced to a set of figures is offensive to many people but there is the further complaint that the simple efficiency of the system represents a potential threat to the individual whose freedom of action might so easily be curtailed by an all-knowing government. For the moment the danger is more apparent than real since the checks and balances of a participating democracy are a fair protection against authoritarian abuses. Those who have a need to protest usually find ways of making their voices heard. That essentially Swedish invention, the Parliamentary Ombudsman, who takes up and investigates complaints by individuals against the activities of the state, has enjoyed such success that he is now supported by the whole group of specialist Ombudsmen. Restrictive trade practices, consumer affairs and press reporting are subjected to their scrutiny. Then, quite apart from the political parties and trade unions multifarious pressure groups see it as part of their responsibility to monitor the exercise of state power.

Of some special interest are the activities of the youth organisations. It may not always be possible to accept their political viewpoint but one can't help admiring their style. Combining grass roots enthusiasm with sophisticated

administrations, bodies like the SSU, the youth wing of the
Social Democratic Party, can have a direct influence on major
policy decisions. 'Political responsibilities *are* taken seriously',
said a young friend and to prove his point showed me a party
pamphlet which contained an extract from the diary of a
nineteen-year-old steelworker and SSU branch chairman.
What about this for dedication to the cause?

Monday. Working party making banners and placards for
the environment demonstration on Saturday. Slogan: Stop
the Chemical pollution – save our lake for swimming.

Tuesday. Committee meeting at the Union.

Thursday. Club meeting. Lecturer from Stockholm
University debating environment protection with the works
doctor.

Friday. Phoned round to SSU and union members about
demonstration.

Saturday. Demonstration a success. SSU member on town
council putting motion for extension of sewage treatment
plant.

Sunday. Walk in the forest with Birgitta.

I was left wondering what Birgitta did for the rest of the
week but information on this matter was not available.

To return to the argument about authority, why, say the
critics, if antidotes are so readily to hand, why is there not a
stronger spirit of opposition to the intrusions on individual
liberty? On one level the answer is in the nature of Swedish
social philosophy. This topic will receive closer attention a
little later but basically, the Swedes find it relatively easy to
assume an air of moderate contentment simply because they
are materially well off.

1 Täby, a new town outside Stockholm.

2. The Wealthiest Nation

Sweden vies with the United States for the first place in the line-up of the richest nations. Currently the Swedes are in the lead, creating more real wealth per head of the population than any other country in the world. Their achievement is based initially on the intensive and intelligent exploitation of natural resources, notably timber and mineral ore, and latterly on the development of advanced technical skills and a very high rate of investment in manufacturing industries such as engineering, pulp paper and chemicals.

Everywhere the age of prosperity is apparent. People are expensively clothed (with a greater emphasis on the smart cut than on imaginative patterns and colours); they drive new cars, go to foreign sun spots for their holidays (in 1974 two and a half million went abroad) and live in luxuriously furnished homes. Flats are the rule even in the smallest towns, a tradition dating from the industrialisation and the rapid growth of urban communities in the late nineteenth century. The demand for simple and cheap accommodation led to the splitting up of houses into apartments and the speculative building of multi-storey blocks of flats. There was nothing fancy about these constructions and any semblance of comfort had to await the arrival of such amenities as running water and proper drainage, not to mention the invention of lifts. But the concept of designing flats to suit the convenience of the residents as much as the penny-pinching demands of the contractors caught on in the 1920s and 30s with the result that the Swedes were soon well ahead with ideas for creating healthier and comfortable homes.

2 With thousands of lakes there is no shortage of waterside picnic spots.

Though lately there has been a shift in preference towards terraced and detached houses, which account for sixty per cent of new accommodation, the most exciting development schemes are associated with communal living. Recognising the problems of social isolation caused by the high rise habitation but reluctant to abandon altogether the environmental economies of the tower block (a Swedish invention of the 1930s), the planners have been working on proposals to improve services for flat dwellers and at the same time to give them a stronger sense of togetherness. Hence, on some of the newer estates the occupants can call on specialists to help look after the children, do the household cleaning or cook and deliver meals. Also it is fairly common practice for block of flats to incorporate indoor play centres and other leisure facilities.

A Swedish flat is compact, but superior design gives it a feeling of spaciousness. Features that might elsewhere be regarded as 'extras' or even luxuries are here part of the standard format. Ordinary families expect and get central heating in every room, double glazing in all windows, parquet floors, and, in the kitchens, which give every appearance of having been designed by time and motion experts, the latest electric cooker, a turn bowl sink unit and a refrigerator and freezer. There is just one deficiency, for which it is difficult to account; the Swedes have yet to discover electric kettles. Perhaps it is simply that the practice of boiling water in a saucepan is the last link with the primitive society and is retained for sentimental reasons. In the same way the Swedes find it impossible to explain why the British tolerate second-rate heating and draughts through every door and window unless it is because they want to be reminded how lucky they are just to have a roof over their heads. The construction of public buildings – schools, hospitals, community centres – continues at a pace which suggests that the planners are having a field day. Everyone in government administration will tell you that money is short but a quick survey of the social services leaves the clear impression that finance is the least of their worries. For example, visiting some schools in the southern county of Kalmar I was shown a science laboratory which looked like the control room at Cape Kennedy, a playground centred nuclear fall-out shelter ('It does very nicely as a table tennis room', said the headmaster) and a junior department art collection valued at £10,000. There is currently vocal criticsm of the glass and concrete jungle created by over-enthusiastic developers. But while everyone can spot the disasters where, to put it charitably, architectural vision has outreached practicabilities, the latest constructions are generally appealing in an uncomplicated sort of way and very pleasant to work in.

Most Swedish families can afford to live comfortably. At 1975 values, average yearly earnings are in the region of £4,000 and a reasonably competent manager or civil servant in his late thirties might feel justifiably aggrieved if he is not making £8,000 to £10,000. Sickness and unemployment benefits are paid up to ninety per cent of income, there are generous family allowances for every child under seventeen and pensions are calculated on the basis of two-thirds of earnings over the fifteen best years. Until recently, the biggest gap in the social services was the failure to provide free dental treatment but that has now been remedied. What is not likely to be changed, despite some criticism from radical groups, is the rule that unemployment pay stops immediately a recipient refuses a job even if it is outside his home area and the principle by which students in higher education are supported not only by grants but by state loans which they pay back when they enter employment.

To attempt to assess family spending power in Sweden, account must be taken of the cost of living which, even bearing in mind recent bouts of world inflation, has climbed on a steep scale over the last decade. The price of food is such that this financially hard-pressed traveller has been known to inquire if the supermarkets offer hire-purchase agreements. The Swedes themselves have a standard joke about their living standards being so high they can't afford to eat, while the reality is that

Swedish food consumption is among the lowest of all industralised nations. The visitor to Stockholm or one of the other larger cities would be well advised not to succumb too often to the culinary delights of the restaurant circuit. A dinner for two in one of the better known eating places can cost twenty pounds or more and with a few drinks before and during the meal the bill can quickly jump the thirty pound barrier. A *Financial Times* comparison of the cost of living for travellers in over thirty cities across the world, calculated on January 1975 prices, put Stockholm fourth from the top. The list was headed by Buenos Aires, Paris and New York. London was twenty-third.

Of some consolation to the resident in Sweden, though not much comfort to the visitor, is the knowledge that accommodation is relatively cheap. Ironically, this is said to be one of the major causes of inflation since controlled rents and house subsidies have increased purchasing power in other areas of the economy. Furniture is also reasonably priced and the visitor who is attracted to Swedish design might think of recouping some of his living expenses by shipping home a few items. There are no import duties on furniture within Europe and while value added tax is payable on the receiving end the Swedish shops offer a corresponding reduction to foreign buyers.

Apart from the cost of living, a major determinant of real income is the tax system, which in Sweden is so sharply progressive as to be almost vertical. A married couple earning £4,500 a year can lose forty per cent of their income on direct taxes and pension and health insurance contributions. With an income of £8,000 the proportion that goes to the government is more like fifty per cent and for £10,000 the figure goes up to fifty-five per cent. It would be too much to say that taxation on this scale is wildly popular, but despite the gloomy forecasts of those who worry about the lack of incentive for individuals to stretch their money-making abilities, there are no obvious signs that the punch has gone out of the Swedish economic drive. And while people complain about not having enough money to spend in the shops, there does not seem to be great enthusiasm for an increase in private spending power if this means a big cutback in public investment.

Industrialisation came late to Sweden. In 1900 nearly sixty per cent of the Swedish people made a living from farming; now the proportion is down to well under ten per cent. The shift of emphasis to industrial production was accelerated by two world wars during which Sweden, as a neutral, conserved and staked up her energy in readiness for the inevitable post-war trade booms. Today about forty per cent of the country's industrial output is exported, most of it to Western Europe. The biggest growth in overseas sales is in the area of manufactured goods, notably engineering products, the sale of which increased by 130 per cent between 1960 and 1968. In the same period the share in the export market of raw materials (lumber, pulp and ores), dropped from thirty-four to twenty-three per cent.

The industry that is more in evidence is forestry, if only because it takes up fifty-five per cent of the land surface. Sweden is the world's foremost pulp exporter and second only to America in the production of fibreboard. Tracking the history of the timber market requires a step back to the Middle Ages when it was realised that money could be made from selling tar and timber to the ship-building nations and providing charcoal for home-based iron smelting. The industrial revolution in Britain set up an increasing demand for sawmilling products which later broadened to take in the export of pulp. The first pulp factory in the world was opened at Bergvik in northern Sweden in 1872. Now, in its latest phase of development the timber industry is concentrating investment in paper production. Just how far technology has progressed in this sector became apparent to me when I visited a mill in Husum in the north-east and saw a recently installed paper-making machine which each year can turn out something in the region of 100,000 tons of exportable produce. The extra labour needed to work this computerised giant totals just twenty-five men. Soon a second machine will be in operation and the managers claim that production will be up to 250,000 tons. I believe them.

Technology has transformed every stage of timber production. The lumberjack is now a machine operator cutting four times more wood each day than his predecessor a generation ago. The skills of logfloating are no longer required because it is cheaper and faster to shift lumber by rail and road. Even the siting of the industry has shifted dramatically since it was realised that the more temperate climate of central and southern Sweden can achieve a much faster growth rate. Now more timber is felled here than in the north and farmers with land that is barely suitable for arable crops, are enthusiastically adapting to a more profitable form of investment.

Another old-established industry is mining – so old in fact it is said that the Swedes were digging iron out of the ground before the birth of Christ. In the seventeenth and eighteenth centuries the country was one of the leading iron producers, thanks largely to the high quality ore mined in the Bergslagen district of central Sweden. What is still one of the biggest mines, Grängesberg, is sited here and although the area has had its ups and downs (the industry all but died when charcoal was ousted by coal) a succession of production techniques based on electric power have ensured its survival as the major iron and steel producing region in Sweden. The ore fields in the north were opened up at the turn of the century after an easy way was found of making steel with pig iron containing phosphorus. The famous mines are Kirunavaara and Luossavaara at Kiruna and Gällivare Malmberget which is a mere seventy miles from the Arctic Circle. Today, the total production from all the mines is in excess of forty million tons.

A high proportion of the top-quality steel produced in Sweden is sold abroad and the country is one of the world's largest exporters of stainless steel. But, Swedish engineering, the growth sector that has taken Sweden into the league of major industrial nations, is also a leading purchaser. The founding fathers of engineering were the inventors. One such was Sven Wingquist who introduced the ball bearing; then, among others, there was L. M. Ericsson who made telephone equipment and Gustav Dalén who introduced automatic beacons and light buoys. The businesses that were set up early in the century to exploit their ideas gave the initial impetus to the development of what, in many cases, are now great international companies. The biggest engineering group – SKF – has subsidiaries throughout the world engaged in machine manufacture. Volvo and Saab-Scania are both well-established in the car and lorry markets (Saab also makes aircraft) while in the area of electrical engineering Electrolux and L. M. Ericsson have reputations that hold good well beyond the domestic market – and the sales figures to prove it.

Sweden is the second largest shipbuilding nation in the world after Japan. Most of the productive effort is concentrated on turning out bulk cargo vessels and tankers. There have been hard times in this industry and competition is always tough but the yards have survived by putting an ever greater emphasis on labour-saving technology. At the Arendal yard in Gothenburg they are building ships on a conveyor belt which carries 300-ton prefabricated sections from the factory out into the dry dock. Engineering is concentrated on the big cities – Stockholm, Gothenburg and Malmö – and employs over a third of the nation's entire labour force.

When analysing Swedish commercial success, foreign observers give much credit to the system of industrial relations which seems to encourage a high degree of co-operation between employers and workers. While other European countries add up the awful cost of output sacrificed to the class conflict, the Swedes, though now experiencing problems with the emerging middle-class unions, generally manage to inject a sense of national purpose into their wage and productivity negotiations. The process by which the increase in national wealth is distributed is based on a forty-year tradition of centralised bargaining between the LO, or Federation of Labour, which represents most of the major unions, the SAF

(Swedish Employers' Federation) and the Government. Periodically the giants hammer out a broad agreement on incomes policy which then serves as a framework for detailed negotiations within each industry. That the system has worked more or less successfully for so long is in part a tribute to the homogenous nature of the Swedish community which instinctively veers away from social conflict. But the desire for consensus is also a product of the delicate balance of political forces which is a continuing feature of Swedish government.

Sweden is a Socialist country in so far as the Social Democrats have held almost continuous power since the early 1930s. But for much of this time Parliamentary majorities have been slender or non-existent, a situation which has compelled successive administrations to temper their policy to suit the needs of one or more of the smaller right-wing parties such as the Farmers (now the Centre Party) or the Liberals. The growth economy, full employment and good public services have been rightly favoured as the ideals most likely to attract support across social boundaries; hence the jibe that Social Democrat ideology has owed more to Keynes and Galbriath than to Marx.

This is not altogether fair comment. As we shall see in a moment in several respects Sweden has moved closer to real socialism than any of the other European countries – including the communist states. But it is true that the traditional left-wing debates on such matters as public ownership have so far played a minor part in Swedish politics. Ninety-five per cent of industry remains in private control, until recently employers retained wide powers or hiring and firing and even now collective agreements have such binding power that most forms of strike action are actually illegal. The unions have kept to a moderate line because they rely on the government to act as a buffer against unreasonable pressures. Curiously enough, the employers, who, of course, view the scene somewhat differently, also look to the government as a last line of defence – against extravagant demands for higher wages.

But all things change and the question now is how long the spirit of co-operation can survive once the emphasis shifts away from the shared objective of economic growth and improvement in material standards. In most countries this would be an academically futuristic line of enquiry; in Sweden, however, the future is not the next decade or the next generation but tomorrow. The working class have achieved the economic breakthrough that is so elusive in other industrialised countries. While the bank manager or lawyer or doctor or business executive is liable to find that progressive taxation puts him on a lower real-income level than that enjoyed by many of his foreign colleagues, the Swedish factory worker is far better off than he would be anywhere else in Europe of the United States. Average working hours are thirty-six in a five-day week as against forty-five in Britain and forty in the United States. Moreover, in Sweden, there is actually a law which forbids any individual to clock up more than 150 hours of overtime in a year. The unions are confidently looking forward to the five-week vacation, though it is interesting that women's organisations are saying that parents and children would benefit more if the six-hour day took precedence over longer holidays.

What next? Well, there is a growing interest in securing better working conditions. This is not to be interpreted as a demand for second helpings in the canteen or clean towels in the washroom; such battles were fought a long time ago. The emphasis now is shifting towards increasing worker interest and participation.

The topical slogans are Job Enrichment, which involves giving the worker greater freedom to decide how to do his job; Job Enlargement, which is achieved by increasing the number of operations that the individual or group has to perform and Job Rotation or the practice of rotating workers round a number of tasks to break the monotony. These ideas are making strongest headway in the car industry where unions and management are keen to get away from the conveyor-belt principle which requires people to act like robots.

At the Saab engine plant at Södertälje, a few miles outside Stockholm, they have done away with the conventional production line; instead groups of workers are each made responsible for assembling complete engines. The new Volvo works at Kalmar is designed to recreate the small workshop atmosphere with groups of up to twenty workers agreeing among themselves on how they will carry out their allotted tasks. Some time is lost, of course, but in terms of hard economics this is more than outweighed by the benefits of having a contented workforce.

On a national level, a law soon to be implemented compels employers to negotiate with the unions before taking any decisions on terms of employment, the method and organisation of work or the choice of machinery or equipment. Employers will be compelled to keep their workers up to date on the profit situation though the Government has stopped short of a trade-union proposal that they should have the right to appoint expert consultants to examine company books. Meanwhile the trade unions have already secured the right to appoint two worker members to company boards and, for its part, the Government is pledged to extend its influence by using the resources of the national pension fund to buy shares in private industry.

All this suggests a leftward swing in the Social Democratic movement. The trend is confirmed by nearly all the current policy debates where the popular theme – some observers would say, the overwhelmingly predominant theme – is the pursuit of social equality.

3. In Pursuit of Equality

It is the concern with equality that has made the Swedes the leading exponents and practitioners of comprehensive schooling. Starting at the age of seven, children embark on a nine-year course which is totally unstreamed until the final year. Learning activities are closely related to the subject preferences of individual pupils who are encouraged to work on their own as much as possible. There is no corporal punishment, no prefects or monitors and the relationship between staff and pupils is easy and relaxed. Some teachers think it is too easy and too relaxed and refer darkly to serious discipline problems particularly in the city schools. But defenders of the new system point out that it would be a miracle if a fundamental change in the concept of school management could be carried through without encountering some oppostion and obstruction from both sides of the classroom desk.

Further and higher education extend to over ninety per cent of those coming out of the comprehensive schools. In the bad old days of unashamed class privilege – everything of two years ago – post-sixteen students were firmly segregated. Those who wanted academic courses, who were usually the children of the professional classes, were on one side of the fence, divided from those who were thought to be more attuned to practical vocational work. Now the entire group attends the integrated upper secondary school where they have a choice of more than twenty lines of study each of which offers a specialist discipline such as economics, technology or social sciences, but also provides a broad-based education so that students do not get too tightly wrapped up in their own little subject parcels.

The expectation is that as the integrated secondary school breaks down the division between academic and practical pursuits, the whole idea of judging occupations and talents against some artificial standard of public worth and prestige will quietly fade away.

Meanwhile the next big push is to be in the area of nursery education – 'an essential element in an educational policy for equality' – because it is here that differences in the home environmental influences can be reduced. The importance of this sector is, if anything, greater in Sweden than in Britain since their school starting age is two years later than our own. At the other end of the age scale, adult education is getting a lot of attention from critics who believe that one of the serious employment and social problems of the future will be the lack of balance between the educational levels of older and younger workers.

For the outside observer the contrast is immediately apparent in the area of general conversation. Young Swedes, whatever their social background or intellectual pretensions, are taught English and most of them speak it very well indeed. Their elders, however, learnt Swedish only or, if they were part of the sophisticated minority, were brought up to accept German as their second language. The distinction leads to social embarrasment since middle-aged Swedes naturally resent the assumption shared by all youngsters that they should appreciate the latest American pop songs or English TV series. More significantly, career prospects can be seriously affected by the inability to communicate in English. Nowadays many of the best jobs are reserved for those who are capable of working efficiently on an international level – and that means being able to converse in an internationally recognised language.

Swedes are by no means inexperienced in the field of adult education. More than a quarter of the total population of eight million are engaged in some form of adult studies. Among the latest reforms is a scheme which opens up certain university courses to anyone over twenty-five who has had five years' job experience even if they have not completed upper secondary school training and lack the usual entry qualifications. But this does not help the socially disadvantaged. The poorest families are naturally worried about possible loss of income and those in heavy industry and on shift work may not have much reserve energy for academic study. About one third of all trade union members claim that their working hours prevent them from taking part in adult education. At the moment the government and employers are considering a recommendation from the trade union movement that all employees should be guaranteed paid leave of absence for general education courses together with incentive payments for undertaking studies in leisure time, free course materials and travel allowances. If these proposals are accepted the Swedes will have moved much closer to their ideal of an 'education system without dead ends'.

Another area in which the Swedes are battling hard for equality is in the relations between the sexes. They would not claim to have invented the idea of sex equality but they were thinking about the question – and coming up with some answers – long before Kate Millett, Germaine Greer and the other stars of women's lib, converted their opinions into best-sellers.

In the early sixties Eva Moberg, the daughter of a Swedish novelist, published an essay called 'The Conditional Emancipation of Women'. Her chief argument – that there would be little progress towards full equality of the sexes until men recognised the need for taking a greater share in the responsibility for raising the family and caring for the home – was taken up enthusiastically by other social commentators.

The economists argued that a continuing improvement in the country's already high living standards depended to a great extent on an expansion of the female labour force. The alternative was to increase the population by encouraging larger families (Sweden has one of the lowest birth rates in the world). But this raised fears of starting a population boom that would get out of hand. In 1960 only twenty-six per cent of married women were gainfully empoyed. But 1965 the proportion had risen by thirty-three per cent. It was a small beginning; just how small was indicated by the forecast of the economist Per Holmberg who calculated that Swedish productivity could be increased by half if the labour potential of women was fully utilised. There were encouraging signs that many more women were eager to escape from the kitchen if they were given the opportunity. One survey showed that there were over 200,000 mothers with children below the age of ten who were ready to go out to work if only they could arrange for their infants to be looked after.

A campaign was got under way to remove sexual discrimination and to establish a fairer distribution of social and economic responsibilities between the sexes. Since it is agreed that the core of the problem is in education, whether in the home, school or college, it is here that the main effort has been concentrated.

The Swedes are not at all averse to using the education system to promote what they regard as a good cause and since school studies are centrally controlled it is relatively easy to change the direction of teaching. The latest secondary school curriculum states unequivocally: 'Schools should work for equality between men and women – in the family, on the labour market, and within society as a whole. They should give instruction on the sex role question and should stimulate pupils to debate and to question the existing conditions'. For some time now it has been the rule in the comprehensive schools that all education be given equally to boys and girls. This applies to such subjects as domestic science and child care. Girls participate in handicraft courses and are encouraged to interest themselves in what were once thought to be exclusively masculine skills like carpentry and metalwork.

There has even been a serious attempt to revise those textbooks found guilty of perpetuating sex prejudice. In the past there have been complaints about books which depict girls as conscientious, dutiful, tidy and helpful, but at the same time passive and timorous, while boys are described as aggressive, disdainful of girls, untidy and forgetful but without any suggestion of reproach being made for these failings. Now, the emphasis is changing. A picture showing mother baking cakes would no longer receive official approval. The last time an illustration like this appeared in a text it was censored out and replaced by drawings which included a kitchen scene with father helping to prepare the breakfast.

The promotion of sex equality was the theme of a big advertising campaign in the schools. One poster which appeared on many notice boards shows a girl smoking a cigar. The caption read 'Girls are not supposed to smoke cigars. What else is it they are not supposed to do?' The answer is in smaller type: 'A girl is not supposed to think she is anything except a girl. A girl is not supposed to take charge of anything A girl is not supposed to care about getting a lengthy education, because she will only want to get married and have children. A girl does not want a technical career, so she should study art, history or literature. These subjects are much more ladylike'. And the punchline: 'The prejudices are many but it is possible to break them.'

The major organisation active in this area is the permanent Sex Equality Commission set up to secure the co-operation of trade unions and the employers. The staff are for ever pointing out areas of discrimination and writing to job advertisers to show them the error of their prejudices – 'They ask for applications without mentioning sex but publish a picture showing only one sex actually doing the job' – and have even been known to protest against Punch and Judy shows because Judy is invariably on the receiving end of violence. The Commission has also acted as a pressure group for better vocational guidance in schools and colleges.

The trouble is that too many careers advisers tend to reflect traditional notions of the sort of employment that is appropriate for boys or girls. One way that has been found to help them adapt their thinking and, at the same time, to open up certain occupations that are either male or female dominated, is the 'sex quota'. This means that if, for example, a boy wants a job as a nursery school teacher or a girl shows an interest in computer programming, they are given preferential consideration.

In at least one important respect Sweden has a head start on most other nations in attempting to establish equality between men and women. All age groups are remarkably free from prejudice in matters of sex relations and are faintly bemused by the failure of other countries to achieve their standard of reasoned toleration. There is a curious paradox here because, as previously noted, the Swedes are rather shy people who are given to formal patterns of social behaviour. Perhaps it is a case of the exception proving the rule. But whatever the reason the establishment feels itself under no obligation to protect the sexes from each other. According to Birgitta Linnér, author of the best seller *Sex and Society in Sweden*, 'We accept sex as a fact of life an feel that men and women, on equal terms, should be free to express their natural sexuality without moral condemnation and social stigma'. Sex education has been a compulsory school subject since 1958. A large and growing proportion of young people have premarital sexual relations (estimates range from sixty per cent to eighty per cent) and the fact causes so little concern that even the Swedish YMCA and the YWCA have been persuaded to merge to form one organisation. Contraception advice is easily available and divorce is a relatively straightforward procedure. In 1974 a parliamentary commission recommended that the remaining restrictions on abortion be lifted so that it can be available to all women who request it.

The latest reshaping of the divorce laws makes clear that adultery is no longer a relevant factor in any court proceedings. At the same time the right of women to share in the distribution of family property is strengthened by the extension of marriage rules to those who live together without formalising their relationship.

3 Glass workers in Småland.

But in other areas of social custom education for sex equality is still having only a marginal influence. Women now constitute one third of the full-time working population but they also represent a majority of the low wage earners. While it is counted as a success that women are beginning to break into traditionally male-dominated jobs such as bus and taxi driving, lathe operating, foundry work and even crane operating, it has to be admitted that little more than one per cent of girls take up technical careers when they leave secondary school. In an attempt to break the circle special training grants are paid to employers who are willing to recruit women to tasks previously dominated by men and vice versa. Moreover, companies obtaining regional development loans or grants must engage both men and women. The rule is that for regional development training, neither sex can be allotted less than forty per cent of training places.

As for the family situation, a recent survey showed that Swedish husbands are typical in so far as they do not show much interest in helping their wives with the household chores. In nearly eighty per cent of families the men contract out of housework almost completely though they are generally prepared to give a hand with shopping and are keen to spend time with the children. On the credit side there is wide support for such reforms as individual income tax which means that families with both members at work will no longer be penalised by high rates of marginal taxation. Married women have the right to receive university or other training and a special allowance while they are doing it. If they do not have the qualifications to enter university, five years working at anything, even housework, is counted as the equivalent. Also, when an employed women has a baby, she or her husband is entitled to seven months leave of absence with pay. If she takes less time her husband can use the rest of her allocation.

This last point raises the question of the future domestic responsibilities of men. Their role, it is argued, must also be transformed if equality between the sexes is to be achieved

4 *The T–bana, Stockholm's subway, is also an experiment in modern art.*

Despite some guffaws from the traditionalists, the expectation is that men will eventually acquiesce because they will realise that the marriage role is as much a problem to them as to women. It is not always pleasing to be thought strong and independent especially when, in reality, men have less latitude than women in determining what they may or may not do. On then to the ideal situation in which men and women can choose freely the roles they wish to perform.

Swedish radical ideas deserve and receive much discussion but it would be wrong to give the impression that all the people enjoy grappling with the social revolution. Right-wing opinion is weakened politically because it is split between three parties but, over the country, conservation is still a powerful force and in everyday life there is much affection for the old values.

For example, the enthusiasm for debating social concepts marks a reluctance to consider change in terms of personalities. In Sweden, the person, and the position he holds, are sacrocanct. Thus, perfectly acceptable and intelligent ideas for running things differently may founder because someone in authority is unwilling to co-operate. The alternative of trying to remove that somebody before he wants to go or before his legitimate retirement age is a prospect that would appal most Swedes. It is a short step from this knowledge to the realisation that society accepts in practice what it dislikes in principle – considerable privilege and status for a select group. This is why the country has a crowned head, albeit one who has no formal powers. But even if the King can no longer select the head of government, attend the weekly Cabinet meetings or even signify his approval to parliamentary bills, he is still honoured as head of state and is much revered by all sections of the community. So much was clear when the quietly academic ninety-year-old Gustav Adolf VI died in 1973 and was succeeded by his young and high-living grandson Carl Gustav XVI. The inevitable change of style in royal proceedings was accommodated by the public without any noticeable loss of enthusiasm for the institution of monarchy. The opinion polls show that over eighty per cent of the nation prefer a king to a president, a statistic acknowledged almost fatalistically by the social reformers. 'Yes. I'm a republican, of course,' said Tage Erlander, when he was Prime Minister, 'But no, I don't think I want a republic.'

More puzzling in a country apparently swinging towards egalitarianism is the wide and continuing influence of a coterie of old-established commercial families. The Wallenbergs, for instance, achieve a billion pound turnover in their various businesses which extend from control of Enskilda Banken, and a major interest in Sweden's top three investment companies, to large shareholdings in seven of the country's international corporations. No less impressive is the staying power of public officials, trade union leaders and politicians. Ther is no suggestion that jobs are handed on within families (at least, not often) but when the holders of particular posts make it seem as if they intend gripping on for ever and inheritance is, in any case, hardly a relevant factor. Tage Erlander was Prime Minister for twenty-two years from 1946 to 1968 and his successor Olaf Palme, though leading a minority government, is generally assumed to be aiming to break the record. As a member of a wealthy upper-class family, married to a woman with aristocratic antecedents, this highly gifted socialist Prime Minister is at the same time a notable example of the survival capacity of the ruling class.

As with old-established politicians so with some old-established political values – they refuse to go away. Consider for instance, Swedish foreign policy which for over 160 years has been guided by a single overriding aim. Sweden spends more on her armed forces per head of population than any Western country other than Russia and the U.S.A., yet she excludes herself from any international agreement that might involve her in military adventure and abrogates the use of force for any purpose except the defence of her own territory. The principles of non-alignment can be variously criticised; but for all those who dismiss the neutral as a parasite on friendly nations who are prepared to fight for a common cause, an equal number recognise the value of an independent and, presumably, objective assessor of the international scene. Or perhaps everyone shifts back and forth from the one view to the other according to the strength of Swedish support for their particular policies.

Certainly the Swedish Government is in no way inhibited from declaring an opinion on foreign affairs. Opposition to the American involvement in the Vietnam War was expressed with such strength that the United States withdrew its ambassador from Stockholm. The country became a popular refuge for American military deserters while the energy of left-wing organisations, particularly those with a strong youth contingent, was devoted to the comfort and support of the 'liberating forces'. The mutual exchange of invective reached its climax when Olaf Palme, the Prime Minister, achieved international notoriety by drawing a parallel between the American bombing raids on Hanoi and the worst of the Nazi war crimes.

This was just too much for some observers who noted that attacks on the anti-communist alliance might be more sympathetically received in the West, if Sweden displayed as much energy advertising the sins of the Soviet and Chinese blocs. The response was to point out the numerous occasions when Swedish influence *was* thrown against the Communists – when Russia invaded Czechoslovakia, for instance, or when Solzhenitsyn was expelled from his country. If Palme was to be criticised for taking an anti-American stand on Vietnam he presumably deserved some praise for describing Solzhenitsyn as 'a symbol for an uncompromising search for truth', a term of respect which, added to a few thoughts on the limiting nature of Soviet freedom, was not well received by the Russian establishment.

Perhaps the most serious criticism of Swedish neutrality (and I quote from a Swedish newspaper) is that 'the willingness of the government to speak out has always been in inverse proportion to the threat of the situation to Sweden itself.' This feeling is most frequently conveyed by the middle-aged and older generations. They remember the bitterness and self-doubt of the Second World War when the policy of non-belligerency was maintained in spite of the Russian invasion of Finland and the German occupation of Norway and Denmark. Neutrality then was more an exercise in pacifying the victors, first of all by trading more or less freely with the Germans and even allowing them to cross Swedish territory en route for Norway, and later, when the Allies were winning the initiative, by responding to pressure to cut off the supply of raw materials to Hitler's war effort. A Swede who was active in the Scandinavian resistance movement once told me of his schocked surprise when, after the war, he discovered that a medal presented to him by King Frederik of Denmark was also being awarded to several of his countrymen who had been unashamedly pro-Nazi until El Alamein.

Swedish nationality has long roots. The last time the country was joined in any sort of military offensive was over 170 years ago when a few Swedish troops assisted in the defeat of Napoleon at Leipzig. Prior to this event a succession of none too glorious defeats had tarnished Sweden's reputation for skilled professional fighting which she had acquired in the great days of Empire – in the seventeenth and eighteenth centuries. Gustavus Adolphus who inherited the throne in 1611 was the earliest of the Swedish conquerors. His excursions into Germany to participate in the Thirty Years' War against the Hapsburg imperialists was a boost for his twin causes – protestantism and patriotism. Sweden emerged as a first-rank military and political power, though Gustavus was killed in battle in 1632. The secret of his success was the formation of a highly trained national army – the first of modern times. Military service was compulsory for all those between sixteen and sixty, weapons and training were improved and standardised and new fighting techniques were developed – notably the salvo which enabled two ranks of musketeers to fire simultaneously and thus with greater effect by applying the simple expedient of having the first rank aim from a kneeling position.

The pursuit of military glory and territorial acquisitions was energetically taken up by Charles X, who extended his rule to the boundaries of modern Sweden and beyond into areas now belonging to Norway and Finland. But the star fighter was Charles XII who, in the space of a twenty-year reign, tackled at various times Norway, Denmark, Poland, Russia, Brandenburg, Prussia, Hanover, England and Saxony. The campaigns though initially triumphant stretched the slender resources of Sweden and the ingenuity of Charles XII to the limit. He was killed in 1718 while leading the siege of Fredriks hald, a fortress in southern Norway. Such was the state of Swedish politics at the time it was suspected, and still is, that the king was shot by one of his own people. At any event his death signalled the breakup of the Swedish Empire which for a short period extended into Germany and Russia.

His successors concentrated their effort on trying to restore to the country some sense of unity of purpose, but while the economy recovered fairly rapidly from the excesses of the warrior kings there seemed to be no chance of re-establishing territorial command of Northern Europe. A succession of ill-judged foreign involvements culminated in war with Napoleon and in 1809 the loss of Finland to Russia. It was at this point that Sweden found herself without an effective ruler, Charles XIII being unwilling to accept any sort of responsibility and, more significantly, not having an heir who could deputise for him. The idea gained favour that it might be wise to elect a crown prince who was favoured by Napoleon. Eventually the choice fell on Jean Baptiste Bernadotte, a Marshal of France who was living in semi-retirement in Paris. He adopted the name of Charles, joined the Lutheran Church and immediately took charge of the country, at the same time making clear that he was not to be counted among Napoleon's camp followers. There was some hope in Sweden that he would lead a campaign to regain Finland, but instead he looked to Norway as a suitable acquisition and, to secure his objective, he allied himself with Napoleon's enemies. The gamble was successful; the two countries were united in 1814 and Bernadotte, soon to be declared king, made the cornerstone of his policy the avoidance of further military entanglements. Sweden has remained neutral ever since and in her political dealings has studiously avoided the use of violence. To illustrate the point, even the eventual break in the constitutional life with Norway which took place in 1905, was achieved without bloodshed and with reasonable goodwill on both sides.

The thought must occur that in skipping lightly over those years of Swedish experience in the aggressive role, no account was taken of that determined company of expansionists – the Vikings. Their most active period was in the ninth and tenth centuries, when their mental skills and expertise in shipbuilding led them into the profitable business of coastal raiding and piracy. But this was not good enough for the Swedish branch of the family. Being better organised and more socially advanced than the other Scandinavian communities, they showed a stronger interest in trade than in plunder. Launching their expeditions from Uppland (already a tightly administered and independent kingdom) and Gotland, the Swedish Vikings ventured into Eastern Europe to mark out trade routes and to set up permanent bases. These colonists who were known as the Ruse, established themselves so securely they were able to maintain their independence well into the thirteenth century and eventually had their name adopted by the country in which they settled. Thus the Swedish Vikings are difficult to categorise. They were not exactly peaceful in their intentions but neither were they conquerors in any sense that Gustavus Adolphus or Charles XII would have appreciated.

Just how effective neutralist diplomacy can be has been proved by the free-trade package negotiated with the EEC. On both sides import duties on most industrial goods and raw materials are to be progressively reduced until finally abolished in mid-1977. The agreement suits both sides admirably but nonetheless came as a surprise to some European politicians who thought that nothing less than fully fledged membership of the Common Market could secure such terms. But then Sweden has had long experience of trade dealings with her continental neighbours. In the immediate post-war years she helped to set up the Organisation for European Economic Co-operation and later, when the idea for a European free-trade area fell through, she joined with Britain, Denmark, Norway, Austria, Portugal and Switzerland to set up EFTA as a counterweight group to the EEC.

At the same time Sweden made the effort to establish a closer relationship with the other four Nordic countries. The great ideal of economic union was abandoned early on because there was no way of persuading the smaller states to forget their fear of domination by Swedish big brother. Still, a Nordic Council was established to explore possible areas of co-operation and there are now several exchange services operating. These include a big cross-boundary movement in electric power, common postage rates and a continuous flow of information on employment opportunities. The most ambitious joint project is SAS – Scandinavian Airlines System – which is funded by Norway, Denmark and Sweden.

While there is no shortage of ideas for future Nordic enterprises any thought of working out some base principles of of unification is politically unacceptable. Nationalistic feelings remain strong and even an outsider can quickly identify important cultural disparities. The jolly and extrovert personality of the Dane is not always compatible with the more reserved and sober nature of the Swede or Norwegian who are themselves divided by the strong element of conservatism which identifies the Norwegian character. Even the languages are wildly at odds. Nobody but the Finns can understand Finnish and when Danes and Swedes get together they invariably give that extra swing to the conversation by talking English.

Today, Swedish forces are internationally active and very

effectively so, but only in support of the peace-keeping operations of the United Nations, an organisation to which the country has given commendable support. Dag Hammarskjöld, who was Secretary General of the UN for eight years from 1953 to his death in a plane crash in Africa, is still revered as the model neutral who was not prepared merely to sit back and watch others fight it out, but instead to act decisively and impartially to create the conditions for a reasoned solution to international disagreements. Swedish influence in these matters is strengthened by a generous and constructive attitude to foreign aid.

4. Design for Living

To return to the subject of traditional values, the Swedes have a strong emotional attachment to folk culture. Annual junketings associated with such rustic celebrations as the coming of Spring, which is greeted with bonfires, and midsummer, when the maypoles are raised, are still treated very seriously indeed. The rule in Sweden is that the eve is more important than the day itself so that, for example, the wildest festivities are reserved for Christmas Eve (when the presents are opened), Midsummer Eve and Walpurgis Eve which is the day before 1 May. On all these occasions and indeed, almost at any party or dinner, folk music is top of the pops. The rousing tum-tiddy, tum-tiddy, tum-tiddy type choruses usually associated with community singing in a German beer garden are belted out from radios and record players.

It all started with the great eighteenth-century poet and lyricist Carl Michael Bellman who, it is claimed, would have the international recognition of Shelley or Goethe, if Swedish was a more widely spoken language. In his home country, however, his imitators and successors have traded profitably on his popularity. Now, hardly a day passes without hearing Evert Taube, the grand patriarch of folk singers, enthusing tunefully about the girls he left behind, and his years as a wanderer, experiences which must by now be distant memories since he has long turned eighty. And if he should tire of performing, there is his son, the popular singer, Sven Bertil Taube, ready to take on the mantle.

Much of Swedish art has a folksy appeal. The work of the

late nineteenth-century artist, Carl Larssom, who depicted in fine detail the humour and pleasures of rustic domesticity, is immensely popular with buyers of prints and postcards. Equally favoured, though evincing a contrasting mood, are reproductions of the little wooden sculptures of Axel Petersson who recorded scenes of abject poverty in Småland – stripped and half starved peasants lining up for the army recruiting sergeant, a village funeral, skinny cattle at market, a bucolic boozing party.

Every town – one is tempted to say, every village – has its craft shop selling textiles, pottery and hand-carved wooden utensils and ornaments. It is a paradox of Swedish life that such a technically advanced country should reserve its highest respect for craft skills. When a Swede has a spare moment his first thoughts turn to weaving a tapestry, shaping a pot or chipping and shaving a piece of wood. Just like old times. The results are sometimes breathtaking but for the outsider it is difficult to keep up to the level of enthusiasm which Swedes appear to feel for all things hand made. One can only guess at an explanation for their passion. For woodcraft, it could be they have acquired or inherited a subtlety of appreciation that is quite beyond anyone who does not live on the edge of a forest. Anyway, no-one should worry if, during a visit, the apparently heretical thought occurs that one wooden fork, or spoon or bowl looks much like another. All foreigners are tempted to say something of the sort and are deterred from doing so by their reluctance to precipitate a fight. But, secretly, we can tell ourselves, we may well be right.

What then of the widely publicised image of Sweden as the country of futuristic styles? It is true that the chief arbiters of popular taste are the professional designers whose adventurous innovations and work with everyday products have influenced the buying habits of all Swedish families. Yet their skills and creative talents are closely associated with the folk tradition. The emphasis is always on individuality both in the creation of an idea and in its application. The highest respect is reserved for the artist who is also a craftsman, capable of carrying his work through to the point where the consumer takes over. Conversely, the crudities of conveyor-belt production are much deplored. But in the age of technological breakthrough and mass demand, the artist/ craftsman is at a terrible disadvantage. He needs protection but not so much that the ordinary shoppers feel cheated of their right to full value for their money. Inevitably the Swedish compromise has been sought and achieved.

The first promise of a creative three-way relationship between manufacturer, designer and consumer came in 1917 when the Society for Industrial Desighn organised a Home Exhibition in Stockholm. The purpose was to show how working-class homes could be structured and furnished in a way that was attractive, practical and inexpensive. Interest was strong but no immediate action followed, for this was at a time when Swedish designers were preoccupied with turning out exclusive high-priced items. But the idea of broadening the scope of design to serve the interest of the entire community was given new life with the take-off of the Bauhaus concept of functionalism in Germany. Thereafter a growing proportion of young designers accepted commissions from industry and concentrated their efforts on developing new froms for household products – clean, smooth lines in furniture, colourful and easily manageable kitchenware, unfussy ornaments. The movement was supported by the big department stores which performed the essential commerical functions of promoting the new standards. Opinion as to what exactly contributes good taste inevitably changed with the generations but economy and functionalism have remained the constants of the Swedish style.

Mostly, production units have been kept on the small side. Of the 600 or so furniture manufacturers, for instance, only twenty-eight have more than 100 employees. Many of these firms are run by craftsmen who became designers before they took up manufacturing. In Småland, a region much favoured by furniture makers, three of the best-known figures in the business. Bruno Mathsson, Yngre Ekström and Karl-Erik

Ekselius, started their careers as carpenters. Hand-made furniture is still available – and when it is of the quality, say, of James Krenov's sideboards and cabinets – exclusiveness is cheap at the price – but as a general rule the touch of originality which is characteristic of so much of Swedish furniture is provided by the close association of imagination and technology.

Nearly all the leading furniture designers have freelance agreements with, or are regularly employed by, the manufacturers. Shape and form are constant topics for discussion both within the business and among consumers. Thus competition is as much about realising the best of the new ideas as about maximising production. When a fresh concept takes off – for instance, tubular steel furniture – there is an immediate rush to improve on the basic idea, to produce better-looking and more practical tubular steel furniture. Elsewhere in Europe (though not in the other Scandinavian countries), the reverse trend still prevails. The old styles have the strongest appeal and when, occasionally, something new breaks the traditionalist line, the manufacturers prefer to imitate instead of trying to go one better. Sadly, this difference in attitudes tends to inhibit Swedish exporters so that the foreign market receives a more than proportionate share of the less exciting items. To see the best of the Swedish furniture it is necessary to visit the country and tour some of the big stores. A good starting point is one of the furniture supermarkets run by KF (the co-operative association) or IKEA. Bearing in mind that this is the lower price end of the market appealing particularly to the young home-makers, the quality is generally excellent. IKEA's own designers produce over seventy-five per cent of what is on sale in their stores.

The basic commercial structure for the furniture trade – fairly small businesses working in close alliance with the designers – applies also to the glass industry. Here again the region of Småland figures prominently. Twenty-eight of Sweden's thirty glass works are here and many of these can date their origin to the days when bringing iron ore out of the swamps was no longer thought to be a paying proposition. From iron smelting to glass blowing was not such a radical shift for a community which had little else going for it except a surplus of timber and a lot of experience in working furnaces. Because Småland was such a poor region, the handicraft tradition took strong root and still influences glass manufacturers to the extent that mass production is regarded as the biggest potential threat to the integrity of the industry. The art and skill of glass making is a topic which recurs in the later pages on Småland but in the context of the present discussion it must be said that the glass designers, both those involved in the production of decorative glass and household items, are among the most radical innovators. It is silly to go in for superlative descriptions because the exciting use of shapes and colours can only be enjoyed if the objects are seen. But as with furniture it is difficult to find a truly representative selection of products outside Sweden. While there is plenty of foreign interest in Swedish glass, prices are said to be too high to allow for large exports.

Those who work with glass are rivalled but not yet threatened by those who work with clay. The famous porcelain factories such as Rörstrand and Gustavsberg are more obviously attuned to mass output but their designers are nonetheless influential members of the production teams. Much effort has been put into the shaping of tableware so that it can be cleaned and stacked easily as well as be pleasant to look at. If achievements in this line are thought to be less significant than what is happening in, say, glass manufacturing it is because so many of the independent designers have sacrificed utilitarian ceramics for the pursuit of pure art.

Now at this point it must be said that, as artists, the Swedes are less than successful. The distinction between the designer and artist may be rejected as artificial – in the Swedish context the terms are frequently regarded as interchangeable – but it is at least arguable that the failures in design are most evident in projects where pure art is more than a nominal factor. The problem is dramatically illustrated in some of the big community building schemes. A new shopping centre, otherwise admirably set out to make life tolerable for the consumer, will display a mess of scrap iron or ill-shaped lump of stone to represent the planners' interpretation of art. Then again the visual impact of a painting or tapestry is often diminsihed by an insistence on communicating some naive message on a political or social theme. A few artists manage to avoid the trap. The sculptures of Britt-Ingrid Persson and Hertha Hillfon are immensely thought-provoking and are justly praised abroad. But the work of those in the second rank, a category which is frantically overcrowded, inspires nothing stronger than a wish that they would stick design.

Similarly with decorative textiles – that other popular art form deriving from the handicraft tradition – the most impressive and lasting effects are produced by those who are essentially designers. Almost every public building of any note has its modern tapestry. Invariably the patterns and colours are stupendous and can be enthusiastically enjoyed for their own sake. But if the tapestry is given a title the chances are that you are then expected to detect some great meaning in what you see, such as, if we all stopped fighting each other the world would be a more loving place. You are left with the impression that somehow, somewhere, art education has missed out on at least one important dimension.

The functional aim of integrating beauty with daily living applies to buildings as much as to their contents. For a long time now the planners have held to the principle that any construction, whatever its purpose, should be pleasing to the eye. If a Swede itemises as early examples of the architectural revolution the Concert Hall in Gothenburg, Stockholm City Hall and – the Rufuse Incinerating Plant at Lövsta, he is not joking. There was a very bad period for Swedish architecture in the 1950s when inspiration from the United States led to the mass destruction of many fine old buildings to make room for glass and concrete boxes. But this lapse in taste which, unfortunately, occurred in a boom time for the construction industry, has been acknowledged and regretted by the authorities. They are now back with what is known as the Swedish Modern or Swedish Grace school of architecture which is committed to the idea of reducing the harshenss of new building. It is achieved by intelligent siting, by the skilful use of colour and by paying proper regard to light and space. And in a country which has amongst its natural resources an immense amount of open land, the possibilities for spacious planning are virtually unlimited.

No apology is needed for giving so much attention to the designers. There is hardly an aspect of Swedish life which has not benefited from their efforts. The popular interest in design has much to do with the Swedish desire to temper the industrial society – to give it some sort of meaning which transcends the strict commercial regard for pace and volume of production. The good designer can suggest ways of improving the efficiency of almost any consumer object. He can also change its looks so that it appeals more strongly as an item of decoration. The principle is perfectly simple and eminently attractive, yet Sweden is one of the few countries to encourage its widespread application.

When the written or spoken word is a component, Swedish art suffers the disadvantage of catering for a minority interest. Sweden is a small country (this is an overworked defence against almost any form of outside criticism – but the fact does have some relevance to the present discussion) and her language is severely localised. Thus in writing, for instance, or in film making it is the rare characters who manage to break the culture barrier and win an international following who achieve fame, fortune and pre-eminence in their discipline. No-one would dispute the quality of the work of numerous artists who are as well-known abroad as at home but there is a strong feeling, especially among the younger intellectuals, that the internationalist group by the very nature of its appeal, tends to ignore or lose touch with matters that are particular to Swedish society. This is not to deny the essential Swedishness of artists like the film-maker Ingmar Bergman or

5 Skiing chalets in Jämtland.

the writer Vilhelm Moberg, (nobody could fail to identify the weighty introspective nature of their work) but simply to say that what they offer is likely to be of marginal relevance to the daily lives of the citizens of, say, Malmö or Kiruna. And if they, the giants of their profession, gave scant attention to specifically Swedish problems what hope have other communicators of stimulating an interest in domestic issues?

Until recently, the immediate and depressing response to that enquiry was so obvious that no-one even bothered to pose the question. But times are changing. Now there is an increasing expectation that the arts can make a stronger contribution to the Swedish debate. This mood of optimism follows a lengthy dialogue between artists and government – the politics of cultural development and the emergence of the state as a generous if sometimes over-powerful benefactor. The policy of supporting the arts by public subsidy raises the problem of securing freedom of political expression. In practice of course, there can be no guarantees. But while the Swedish establishment may not be too keen on the wild eccentricity that may occasionally set off a spark of genius, there does seem to be sufficient checks and balances in the system to ensure that a wide range of ideas are acknowledged and respected.

The nature of state support extends all the way from individual awards and scholarships to the purchase of art for public buildings. Working facilities are provided, events sponsored and information distributed. To take a particular example film making relies on public subsidy to an extent that without it the industry would fall apart. The scheme is based on a ten-per-cent levy on box office receipts which is supplemented by about half as much again by a government grant. Financial control is with the Swedish Film Institute which distributes funds or loans to encourage new productions and supports a film school to train directors' cameramen and technicians. A few expensive mistakes have been made by directors whose self-confidence outweighs their ability but at the same time new and exciting talents have

6 *Christmas shopping in Gothenburg.*

moved into the limelight and no one questions that films are being made which say something constructive about, and to, society. The critical appraisal of the Swedish ideal contained in such films as 'I am curious, yellow' and 'I am curious, blue' (directed by Vilgot Sjöman) has even made an impact on foreign audiences though their box office appeal may be more closely linked to the promise of explicit sex than to an interest in political analysis.

Generally, the following of the Swedish film abroad has been disappointing although the point made earlier about relating content to matters of direct consequence to Swedish audiences is bound to limit the appeal of many productions. The pity of it is that in rejecting story lines that are apparently confined to a minority culture, foreign distributors are depriving cinemagoers of the chance to assess new styles of directing which are every bit as exciting as anything from the American or mainstream European film output. Ingmar Bergman, of course, can still charm the box office and the films of Mai Zetterling, though critically underrated, have travelled the major circuits. Then there is Jan Troell who is responsible for the two-part epic (an unusual word in Swedish film language) based on the Vilhelm Moberg books collectively known as *The Immigrants*. His twin films, which run for three and a half hours each, follow the lives of a mid-nineteenth-century farming family on the trek from the poor lands of Sweden to the potential riches of the American mid-west. Foreign critics have praised the superb camerawork (Troell is his own cameraman and editor) which picks out detail in a way that enhances the sense of realism. But participation in what seems to have been a constant round of daily suffering can be tough going for audiences who are accustomed to frequent interludes of light relief.

Troell's undoubted abilities have made him a Swedish export for he is now directing English-language films in the United States. It will be interesting to see if his talent survives the change of environment. From the acting side few have taken the journey without losing something on their careers.

An honourable exception is Ingrid Bergman. As for Greta Garbo, well, who knows what she might have achieved in different circumstances? But among the more recent recruits to international stardom, Bibi Anderson has not so far fulfilled the promise of her Swedish (Bergman) films and Max von Sydow, though by any standards one of the greatest actors, somehow always manages to reserve his finest performances for the Swedish screen and stage.

State backing is as important to the theatre as to the cinema – possibly more so, since the principle of subsidy has for much longer been associated with the live arts. The Royal Opera, which is also the home of Swedish ballet, was founded and financially supported by Gustav III, one of the most cultivated of the eighteenth-century European monarchs, whose other achievements included the setting up of the Royal Academy. But his attempt to secure political ascendency was less successful than his efforts to achieve cultural rejuvenation. His opponents, hoping to put a block on their slide into obscurity, plotted his assassination, which was carried out one evening when he was attending a masket ball at the Royal Opera. Appropriately, the event inspired a play by Strindberg and an opera by Verdi.

The Royal Dramatic Theatre has shared in the traditional support for the arts from the ruling family and the state. Throughout the nineteenth century it was linked to the Opera by a joint management and today, though once again an autonomous institution, it is bound to recognise, as one of the conditions of subsidy, that the two bodies should work in close co-operation. A liberal range of performances includes many foreign plays. Of the Swedish classics, pre-eminent is the work of August Strindberg whose penchant for savage self-analysis has inspired a succession of soul-searching dramatists. Henrik Ibsen, though suffering from the slight disadvantage of Norwegian parentage, receives hardly less attention.

Though based in Stockholm, the Royal Opera and the Royal Dramatic Theatre, bravely attempt to create a national appeal. Productions go on tour and there is a regular interchange with the provinces of performers and directors. But cities of the stature of Gothenburg and Malmö, which are proudly independent, have their own state-subsidised theatres and repertory companies, not to mention their own orchestras and concert halls. Competition with Stockholm is intense and the quality of their productions is strictly comparable to the standards of performance in the capital.

On the literary side the government has recently decided to fund the publication of books written by Swedes in Swedish. The idea was put up in response to rising costs which have made all but the most expensive minority interest books totally uneconomic. Unfortunately, it is one of the problems of the Swedish culture that everything published in that language is, by definition, of minority interest. It is hard enough for an American or British writer to attract interesting his first book but in Sweden where the number of potential readers is so much smaller, it is even more difficult to persuade the publishers and the booksellers to risk money on a beginner. From their point of view it is far easier and economically safer to translate the work of established American and European writers whose international reputation guarantees them a head start in capturing the Swedish market.

Books in Sweden are expensive and, indeed, it comes as some surprise to learn that along with other consumer products, they bear VAT. But the problem of encouraging Swedish writers cannot be solved simply by abolishing the tax and lowering the general price level in the shops. As the publishers are first to admit, this would serve only to boost the number of translations and to swell the incomes of foreign authors. The alternative is a selective subsidy to the publishers of the better-grade Swedish literature. The question here, of course, is who decides what is or is not good-quality writing. It could be that to rely on the consensus opinion of committees of respected cultural experts is to play safe and promote the thoughts and attitudes which accord with establishment opinion. On the other hand, it is undoubtedly better to face this issue and the risks involved than to have no home-produced books at all.

One reason for anticipating that the subsidy issue will eventually work out to the satisfaction of most writers and publishers is that the state already has good experience in supporting the written word. For instance a Swedish author is paid a small fee every time one of his books is borrowed from a public library. The sums involved are about 2p for an ordinary reading book and 8p for a reference volume. Not all of this goes straight into the writer's pocket since more than half is set aside as a contribution to the 'free' account which provides for authors' pensions and working and travel grants. In this way the really popular writers whose books are widely borrowed contribute most to the general well-being of their profession.

That Sweden retains the highest readership of daily newspapers anywhere in the world must have something to do with the recently introduced practice of using a tax on the advertising revenue of the big papers to support the less prosperous section of the industry. The yearly total of government aid to the press is well over fifteen million pounds with the bulk of this money being paid directly to the smaller provincial newspapers. The rest is allocated in the form of value-added-tax exemptions and postal subsidies. An interesting fact for those who doubt the capacity of any government of whatever political colour to act impartially in the matter of handing out financial aid, is that among those newspapers receiving the largest awards is a representative selection controlled by the Conservative, Liberal and Centre parties.

With such apparently easy access state funds, it is surprising that not more effort is made to liven up the television service, which gives every impression of being operated on the cheap. It is not that individual performers or directors are lacking in talent as compared with their European colleagues – if anything, the reverse is true – but it is impossible not to believe that their impact would be greater if they had larger studios and a few more cameras to work with. Perhaps with limited resources they attempt too much. Of the programmes shown on the two channels, by far the highest proportion is made in Sweden. Few of these have a market abroad, a fact which inevitably effects budgets, but conversely, the Swedes are disinclined to economise by importing many of the cheaper foreign programmes. For the visitor, watching Swedish television is to experience a welcome release from the antics of tough-guy detectives and trigger-happy cowboys. But after a while the faithful viewer begins to wonder if there is not too much reliance on the standard political interview, the studio discussion and the educational documentary.

It has been suggested that the financial state of Swedish TV could be transformed by the opening of a commercial channel. But opposition to advertisements on television and radio is virtually unanimous and there is much contempt for the infantile level of programmes which is said to characterise sponsored broadcasting. Another possibility for brightening the evening hours (and in winter they certainly *need* brightening) is to introduce into television a stronger element of comedy. But perhaps this is asking too much. The Swedes enjoy a good joke as much as anyone but their humour is somehow a private matter reserved for conversation with family and friends. Raucous and uninhibited mirth is not part of their nature. Anyone who doubts this should try laughing out loud in a cinema or theatre. An equivalent social gaffe in Britain would be to throw ice cream over the balcony.

Interpreting culture in its broadest sense, as a way of life, the Swede who has had greatest success in projecting his country's ideals on to the international scene is undoubtedly Alfred Nobel. The Nobel Prizes, allocated yearly to outstanding achievement in science, literature and peace-making might best be described as awards for the structured pursuit of excellence.

It is not simply that three fifths of the prizes go to scientists (after all Nobel was himself a scientist of considerable note), but judging by the back list of winners, the men and women who are picked out for commendation invariably hitch their claim to a reputation for order and clear-sighted management of their talents. It is not so much genius as perseverance that is acknowledged. Perhaps this is in large measure an inevitable concomitant of administering any academic award scheme, let alone one of world stature. But it also reflects the Swedish regard for those who achieve success by dogged application.

Regarding the Nobel Laureates from this viewpoint, it is not then so surprising to find among the literary champions such second-league players as Rudyard Kipling, Romain Rolland, Anatole France, Sinclair Lewis, John Galsworthy, Pearl Buck, François Mauriac and Winston Churchill. Occasionally, the judges let their hair down, latterly with their awards to the Russian dissidents Boris Pasternak and Alexander Solzhenitsyn. Even here the thought occurs that though these writers are unquestionably interesting, can it really be that they are literary world beaters? But for all their limitations, which given human imperfection, will never entirely disappear, the Nobel Prizes are much sought after. Backing their immense prestige is the added appeal of their financial value which at present averages a little over £55,000 for each prize.

The origin of the Prizes is the will of Alfred Nobel, a chemist who proved his creative ability by inventing dynamite and several other forms of high explosive. He was also an accomplished and very rich business man who set up throughout Europe manufacturing companies which were the forerunners of such conglomerations as ICI and Société Centrale de Dynamite. Without family or even many close friends for whom he felt any personal responsibility he determined that, after his death, his fortune would be devoted exclusively to improving the general lot of man by extending the boundaries of knowledge and ideas. His will specified that his companies should be sold and the money invested in gilt-edged securities – an unfortunate decision in many ways since the value of the capital fell drastically during the inter-war period of inflation. The interest on the investment was to be distributed yearly in the form of prizes to those who had 'conferred the greatest benefit on mankind', in the fields of physics, chemistry, physiology or medicine, literature and international brotherhood. The will was signed in November 1895, Nobel died the following year and the first prizes were awarded in 1901.

One of the curiosities of the Nobel Awards is that the adjudication of the prize which attracts the strongest popular interest – the Peace Prize – is the responsibility not of any Swedish authority but of a committee elected by the Norwegian Parliament. The anomaly was created unwittingly by Nobel who, in nominating the institutions to administrate the project, did not take account of the possibility that Norway and Sweden, then united, might subsequently drift apart. The recognition of Norwegian independence in 1905 did not affect the terms of the will and Norway has continued to exercise her prerogative, though not always in a spirit of brotherly accord with her partner and neigbbour. Unhampered by a philosophy of strict neutrality and an inherent mistrust of big-power politics the Norwegians have sometimes bestowed honours which have offended and angered the Swedes. When in 1973 the Peace Prize was awarded to Henry Kissinger and Le Duc Tho for their efforts in negotiating a short-lived cease fire in Vietnam, a leading Swedish newspaper reported the news under the heading 'The War Prize'. There was a widespread feeling that the Nobel Foundation had been discredited by association with those who sought peace only when it was clear that a war policy was failing to achieve its objectives. There were calls for the resignation of the award committee and a guarantee that in future the Peace Prize should be given only to those who are against solving conflicts by by force, not only occasionally but in general.

But personality disputes are not limited to the Norwegian sector of the Nobel Foundation. The Swedes also have their difficulties in securing general consent for their nominations. The major problem centres on the changing nature of scientific investigation. The days of the dedicated genius giving over his life to the lonely pursuit of a single hypothesis are long since over. Today, all is teamwork which means that it can be near impossible to pick on one person who is worthy of the awards. The compromise had been to offer a prize to two or more scientists involved on a particular project but even this can lead to internecine squabbles. Then again, the overwhelming proportion of awards have so far reflected cultural advancement in the Western Hemisphere. With the latest shift in the balance of world politics, such a one-sided view of progress is no longer permissible. But where are the judges qualified to assess the relative value of Asian scientific and literary achievement? Who will be the first to dare to nominate a Chinese writer for the Nobel Prize for Literature?

5. Food and Drink

Whenever a Swede has a spare moment he either weighs himself or measures his waist. The accuracy of this statement (including the use of personal pronoun) can be proved quite easily without an involved and possible embarrassing inquiry into the private lives of your Swedish friends. Simply walk into the nearest supermarket and glance along the shelves of dairy produce. You will find low-fat margarine, low-fat cheese (labelled clearly and proudly in the way that in many other countries full-fat cheese is advertised) low-fat yoghurt and a profusion of other slimming foods. The other sort of nutrition is, of course, readily available but a spot check of the shoppers choice gives a clear impression that the nation is trained to live on a non-fattening diet. Sweets are not sold in great quantities and to be offered a meal which contains an excess of sugar or stodge is a rare occurence.

Curiously, the Swedes strict regard for healthy eating does not extend to the other Scandanavian countries. The Norwegian and Danes have a passion for butter, eggs, cheese, milk and large creamy cakes while the Finns who enjoy all this and also smoke heavily have, as a result, set a world record – in the numbers dying from heart disease. But one thing all of these people have in common is that they enjoy their food. The Swedes, for instance, have perfected the art of raising the appetite by offering a salty bite of anchovies or pickled herring washed down with a gulp of schnapps (preferably the superb 'Skåne' brand). What comes after that depends on the season of the year and the region in which you happen to be staying. As a general rule, however, the Swedes go for hot heavy soups and casserole dishes in winter and elaborate salads in the summer.

Far and away, the most popular national dish is the Smörgåsbord which is best described as an attempt to transform an hors d'oeuvre into a multi-course meal the old days it was simply a pickled herring appetizer which preceded a big festive dinner. Then more and more dishes were added – cheese, potatoes, eggs, cold and hot meats and even fresh fruit salad. The idea is to take an empty plate and to go on an extended tour of the food table picking out a bit of this and a bit of that. You can return to the smörgåsbord as often as you like, assuming that you can drag yourself across the floor after the first two or three helpings, so instead of trying to accommodate every item on the first round, adopt the Swedish example and establish an order of priorities. Go first of all for the centrepiece of the show – the herring dishes, which are generally served with sour cream, finely chopped chives and hot boiled potatoes. The Swedes have discovered all sorts of ways of salting, smoking and pickling the herring and though sometimes the results are a little strong for the uninitiated taste, the sharpest tang can usually be washed away with plenty of schnapps and beer. The exception is surströmming, a Baltic recipe which can only be translated as rotten herring. To anyone not brought up in the northern forests the smell of this exotic food is similar to and about as appealing as a gas leak in a damp cellar. But fortunately for the newcomer to the smörgåsbord, the chances of encountering surströmming are remote. The Swedes are rapidly losing their taste for a food which could justify itself only when there was little else available to eat throughout the long winter months.

After the smörgåsbord herring comes another selection of fish courses – cold smoked salmon, perhaps, or anchovies, the tiny sprats caught off the west coast which are quite unlike the Mediterranean variety. Then on to the cold meat courses such as pâté, sliced beef, smoked reindeer, or one of the varieties of Swedish sausage which range from soft and thickly sliced salami to medvurst or smoked sausage which is served with sweet onions and pickled tomatoes. Choose small helpings because sausage can be fattening and it would be ungracious to set a bad example to your hosts who are doing their best to keep control of their culinary passions. Anyway, you should leave room for a hot course, the choice of which will undoubtedly include Jansson's Temptation, a heavily spiced potato-based dish famed for its overpowering effect on anyone brought up on plain food, and meatballs which are said to be not quite so good as those every Swedish mother *used* to make. Finally, there is usually a fruit salad or cheese to round off the meal.

The smögåsbord does not exhaust the possibilities for enjoying Swedish food. In Skåne, the rich southern agricultural region where they pride themselves on eating well, they serve fine home-made pâté and sausage. Another local delicacy is smoked eel. But the meal which is savoured with the loudest lip smacking by the farmers of Skåne is the Michaelmas goose, eaten throughout the closing weeks of the year but particularly associated with St Martin's Day or Mårten gås. It is of some satisfaction to those who enjoy this annual feast that Bishop Martin of Tour is the patron saint of the art of cooking. Goose parties are common to most regions in the south but it is only in Skåne or places where Skåne people have infiltrated that you are likely to encounter that extraordinary starter to the main course known as black soup. It is made, or so I am reliably informed of goose innards boiled in pig's blood. If black soup does happen to be included in your menu the best advice is to eat quickly and try to think about something else. From those who will try anything a few times comes the additional invaluable tip that the liquid is least offensive to the palate when served very hot.

In nearby Småland and Öland the speciality is Kroppkakor or dumplings containing chopped pork. It is an old-fashioned recipe which has recently lost favour with weight-conscious Swedes but it is still possible to encounter families for whom nostalgia and a tasty meal are more important than the latest diet. Rather more easily sampled is the Småland cheese cake which is identified by the almonds embedded in its firm texture. It is served with cream and raspberry jam.

At the northern end of the country good popular eating is associated with smoked reindeer meat. It is at its best when served with one of the many different types of flat bread, which is usually pancake-shaped and is made in varying degrees of crispness. This bread – or perhaps one should say 'these breads' because the only thing they really have in common is that they are essentially Swedish – can be bought all over the country, but the recipes originate in the north and it is there that the finest baking is concentrated. Or so they say. A delicious follow-on to smoked reindeer or any of the salty dishes so favoured by the Swedes is cloudberries and cream. Cloudberries are unique to Sweden and it is not easy to suggest a comparable taste except say they are a bit like raspberries but orange in colour and much lighter and smoother. They can be picked wild in the northern forests where they grow on the soft damp patches of grounds which sometimes break the tree line. Or they can be bought in the food shops in the south but at such a price it might be thought more economical to find a large basket and to catch the first train up country.

The north-east coast brings a good fish harvest. A favourite summer sport among holiday makers and weekenders is casting a net for strömming or sprats which are then grilled and served as part of a beach picnic. Salmon – marinated or smoked – is also popular especially when eaten with crisp bread. A greater variety of sea food is caught on the warmer west coast, but in this region and throughout the south it is the freshwater crayfish which hold the undisputed lead in the ranks of gastronomic delights. Crayfish look like prawns but are about three times as large. They are in such demand that fishing is restricted to part of August and September so that the species should have a reasonable chance of replenishing its numbers in time for the next season. One of the happiest experiences in Sweden is to attend a crayfish party held in the warm open air of a summer evening. But the centrepiece of the feast can go to waste if no effort is put into learning the special suck-and-chew technique for extracting the luscious juice and meat.

Some of the most distinctive Swedish foods are associated with annual festivals. St Martin's goose dinner is one example. Then there is the cream and almond bun eaten just before Lent, which is light enough to be served floating in a bowl of warm milk (seriously!). At Christmas boiled or roast ham, is the principal dish and on Christmas Eve many families go through the ritual of 'doppa it grytan' which is to eat bread dipped in the stock from the boiled ham. For the traditional Christmas Eve dinner they start with an elaborate and rich Smögåsbord with sausages of every shape, size and taste, herring, pâte, pigs' trotters and spare ribs. This is followed by a main course called Lutfisk or cod first dried and then boiled and made very tasty by adding white sauce heavily spiced with black pepper. Anyone who has stomach space left can top up with a rice porridge and milk.

Since the biggest meal in Sweden is saved for the evening, lunch is very light and brief affair, usually little more than an open sandwich. But breakfast is substantial enough even if it is what the British call a continental-style beginning to the day. A hotel will offer several choices of cereal, eggs, cheese, toast or bread and jam (but rarely marmalade) and pure fruit juice which is regarded as a life saver by every early riser. The Swedes brew excellent coffee but they also happen to believe that it is possible to make a decent cup of tea by pouring luke warm water on to a miniature tea bag. They are wrong.

If you do have trouble in holding out to the evening for the big meal it is easy enough to pick up a snack at one of the many Korv bars. These are a bit like hot-dog stands but cleaner and generally more appealing. You can buy Varm Korv (frankfurters) with chips of mashed potatoes and enough sauces and pickles to fill a plate twice over.

The Swedes are as restrictive about drink as they are free about sex. Alcohol is *the* great national hang-up. The temperance organisations, founded in the mid-nineteenth

century, remain wealthy and influential; social and medical
workers give much of their time to combating excessive
drinking (though it is difficult to imagine how anyone can
afford to be an alcoholic in a country where a bottle of whisky
or gin is priced at nearly £8) and the newspaper moralists are
forever complaining of the extent of public drunkenness –
which is almost certainly a good deal less than in most
European countries. Where else (except Norway) would you
find a group of students arguing with ferocious intensity – not
on the future of capitalism or the promise of world peace – but
on the comparative danger to health of a glass of brandy and a
large scotch.

Until 1955 alcohol was on ration. Men were entitled to four
litres a month; single women, half that amount and married
women – nothing at all. Attitudes are said to be more liberal
nowadays though any foreigner approaching one of the state
monopoly liquor shops might be forgiven if he thought he was
committing an illegal act merely by walking into the place.
These establishments, of which there are only 300 in the entire
country or one to every 28,000 citizens – are dingy and
depressing as a prohibition-era booze palace. Decorated, if
that is the word, in dirty brown and dull grey, the selling area
is usually a single open room flanked by a long bar. The
bottles lie in racks behind the bar safely out of reach of the
patrons who, far from contemplating any rash act, keep their
eyes down and give every indication of not wanting to be seen
by their friends. The shop assistants have the appearance of
being trained in funeral parlours. On the top of each cash
register is a red light and when it flashes, as it does at irregular
intervals, the customer who is at the head of the queue is
required to show his identity card. The purpose of this
exercise is to check whether the prospective purchaser is below
age or on the black list of alcoholics or is otherwise prohibited
from touching the hard stuff.

But the liquor shops are not entirely beyond redemption.
There are, for instance, some bargains in good quality wines –
not so cheap that a Frenchman or Italian would be impressed

but reasonably priced by Swedish standards. The credit for keeping down costs, despite a high luxury tax, belongs to the Swedish Liquor Monopoly. As the biggest wine and spirit wholesaler in the world it can extract preferential terms for its purchases which currently total some forty million bottles a year. But how can Swedish commercial acumen which, in this case, is building a growth market for booze, be reconciled with the power of the anti-drink lobby? As always in Sweden the answer is – compromise. The demand for wine is stimulated, but not too much. How far this almost schizophrenic desire to pursue two contrary objectives can be taken was indicated recently by a popular advertisement which advised 'Wine is good for you – but not every day.'

More reasonably priced than imported spirits are the traditional Swedish hard drinks such as schnapps which is knocked back early in a meal with the herring or anchovies or some other salty starter, and punch, a heavy liqueur-type drink savoured hot with winter soups or ice cold with after-dinner coffee. Hot liquor is naturally much favoured in the winter months which is why one of the inevitabilities of the season is a succession of Glögg parties. Glögg, a red spicy wine, is tastiest when served with whisp of steam rising from the glass. The food at such gatherings consists of a few nuts and sultanas which are allowed to soak in the wine to bring out its full flavour and ginger biscuits and saffron buns which are eaten independently. The general mood of wellbeing evident at all these parties can be enhanced if the glögg is strengthened with vodka or schnapps.

Beer, the most popular drink in Sweden, is produced in four different grades. Those with the lower alcoholic content can be bought in the supermarkets but choose carefully to avoid the weakest category which is likely to appeal only to those who favour the consumption of mild detergent.

7 *A fishing village in Bohuslän.*

6. The Complete Traveller

Sweden has nearly all the advantages needed for a prosperous tourist industry – recreational facilities are varied and of good quality, hotel or chalet accommodation is plentiful and the wide open spaces for which the affluent European city people yearn are here an accepted part of the national heritage. The population per square mile is 45 against 586 in Britain and 624 in West Germany. Even the climate, which one might assume to be unhospitable in a country which is roughly on the same latitude as that of Alaska, is saved by the warm air of the Gulf Stream. A good summer can stretch from May to September and the best holiday months June and July are hot, light and dry. The midnight sun is reserved for the sector north of the Arctic Circle but everywhere in the north the evenings are long and bright. Summer temperatures vary little between north and south.

November is a horrible month – cold and wet – with the night closing in before the end of the afternoon – but the crisp snow of winter can be appealing and not just to skiers and Lapps. The Swedes believe in keeping warm, and central heating wherever you go, even under main street pavements, can take the edge of the sharpest spell. In the far north an average of 217 days a year are below freezing while in the south the figure is not much above 50.   In January and February the entire length of the country is a playground for the winter sports' enthusiasts. By March, those in the far south have put away their skis and skates but in the centre and the north the season can extend well into April.

A curious fact about the landscape is that it is invariably

8 *The Trollhättan Locks on the Gota Canal.*

dominated by water. There are said to be 96,000 lakes and if that sounds an awful lot I can only add my opinion that the civil servant who did the calculating lost count somewhere along the way and underestimated the total. Remembering the 4,000 miles of coastline, it must be apparent that Sweden is nature's gift to sailors, swimmers and, in winter, skaters.

All in all, an ideal choice for a holiday – except for one thing: Sweden is not frantically keen on tourists. By saying this I am not invalidating the point made earlier – facilities for holiday makers *are* good – it is simply that not much effort is made to attract visitors from abroad. Tourism provides less than two per cent of Sweden's foreign earnings and with the closing down of several tourists offices in Europe it is clear that even starting from the low base line it is one industry which is not likely to break any records for economic growth. The big fear is that what is special to the Swedish scene, the chance to move about without forever tripping over your fellow humans, could be irretrievably lost if the place becomes say, another Spain. The danger may seem to be exaggerated but the Swedes are more conscious than most of potential and actual threats to environment and are wealthy enough to afford not to take any risks.

One consequence of this attitude is that it can be difficult to arrange a suitable holiday package deal.

The big Scandinavian shipping lines such as Swedish Lloyd, Tor and Fred Olson offer a limited range of moderately priced inclusive tours. But Scandinavian Airways is averse to charter flights to Sweden and, by the rules of international aviation, has the power to stop other companies offering cheap rates. At present an ordinary return fare from London to Stockholm in the spring and summer months is nearly £200. Fares to Gothenberg are slightly cheaper and savings are possible by booking three months ahead or on night flights. A few determined souls claim to have achieved mighty economies by aiming for Norway or Denmark and then connecting with local schedules. But what with the involved planning effort and the time spent hanging about in airport lounges travelling can become a protracted and tedious affair.

On the other hand, the shipping lines make a virtue out of a leisurely journey by offering attractive prices and, assuming a smooth crossing, reasonable comfort. Another credit for the sea trip, at least on the shorter routes, is the use of the car ferries. Hiring your own vehicle opens up the possibility of exploring parts of Norway and Denmark as well as Sweden but if this is thought to be too ambitious bear in mind that in land area, Sweden is one of the big Europeans and that sight-seeing even in a single region requires easy mobility. This is not to malign the rail and coach facilities which are almost certainly superior to anything most of us have previously experienced, but their best value is the main-line services and the last thing a visitor wants is to be restricted to the towns.

The Swedish State Railway (SJ) has about 15,000 kilometres of track which is nearly all electrified. There are two classes of compartment on the trains but the standards of comfort and service are such that most travellers are very happy to accept what is offered for a second-class ticket. For the holiday periods seats need to be booked well in advance and to be on the safe side, a sleeping berth should be reserved at least six months ahead of the day of your journey.

Incidentally mention of the railways is a reminder that while everyone agrees they are comfortable and efficient, few realise they are the product of one of the first efforts in Swedish economic and social engineering. The major constructional effort was in the 1870s when it was agreed that the state should build and operate the trunk lines while private enterprise should control the branches. The result of this policy was that the state held overall control even when it owned only a third of the lines. Moreover, railways were planned to take industry into the poorly developed areas where good transport was needed to attract industry.

By these standards, the development of the road system has been less successful. Until recently the emphasis was on construction in the affluent south, at the expense of the north, where many of the secondary roads are still not much better than dirt tracks. Still, overall the road network is a thing of joy for every visiting motorist. That magic social formula – a small population over a large territory – makes traffic holdups a rarity for all except Stockholm's weekend commuters. Even where motorway building is only a promise, and in parts of Sweden this form of travel is still regarded as a novel innovation – the chances are well in favour of maintaining good cruising speeds. Probably for the same reasons road services are generally of an excellent standard. Cafeteria meals are actually quite appetising and easily available. Frequent clearly designated picnic and camping spots are maintained with such care that even the British tourist might think twice before spreading his litter over the grass.

Driving is on the right. This may seem an obvious point but some visitors still hold to the belief that the Swedes share wit the British the idiosyncrasy of keeping to the left. In fact the great changeover took place in 1967 – an event which made motoring history, not least because all traffic was stopped for six hours and then drivers were compelled to limit speeds to under thirty miles an hour during a three-day transitional period. That this exercise in self-restraint was an immense success (the accident rate was lower than in an ordinary week) suggests, rightly, that the Swedes are cautious motorists. Road signs are rigorously obeyed and a recommendation to keep headlights on during the day is generally observed. The value of this custom is self-evident when the weather is bad and few cars are on the road, but in normal conditions blazing lights can be disconcerting particularly for the unitiated foreign driver who thinks he is being warned of some terrible danger ahead.

The police are friendly but are quite capable of issuing on the spot summonses for minor infringements of the traffic law. Thus, do not sound your horn in built-up areas unless you are faced with an emergency. The proper way to attract another motorist's attention is by flashing headlights. Do not drink and drive. With their views on the evils of alcohol the Swedes are disinclined to be merciful with the woozy driver even if he does happen to be a socially deprived foreigner. And it is no use grinning pathetically at the road cop and telling him you do not speak Swedish. He will cheerfully assure you that language is no problem because *he* speaks English.

Parking regulations vary from one city to another. In Stockholm and other cities they have a handy rule for those who want to leave their cars on the street overnight. If tomorrow's date is an even number, parking is allowed only on the side of the street with even-numbered houses; the following day everybody moves over to the odd-numbered side. Parking is also forbidden just one night in the week. Since fines for breaking the rule are heavy it is wise to check the local regulations at the outset of a visit.

When a Swede talks about distances in miles he is assuming his own definition of the measurement. This fact can take on a frightening significance if you want to get somewhere on time and forget that the Swedish mile is six times longer than the British mile. On the roads the risk of misunderstanding is slight since all signs are marked up in kilometres. In the summer months Swedish radio three provides an evening news summary and weather forecast in English and German – a useful service to the traveller but one that is not easy to publicise. Another bonus is that whenever there are instructions for using the telephone, an English translation is posted alongside. This can be a great consolation to a stranded driver but, remember, there are no motoring organisations in Sweden willing to dash to the rescue, and apart from self-service petrol, garages are generally closed in the evenings and weekends. In other words if you suffer a breakdown outside working hours, you are on your own.

Another cautionary thought; the Swedes have strict rules against roadside advertising, which is happy news for those who like to forget the pressures of the consumer society (who can remember travelling mile after mile without sighting even a solitary billboard) but is less appealing for motorists who expect the places and events worth visiting to be clearly and frequently signposted. On Swedish roads it is no use looking for pointers to historic monuments, exhibitions, parks or whatever. The best they offer is town signs (almost always the same in English as in Swedish except for Gothenburg which in the home language comes out as Göteborg) and occasional tourist information maps posted discreetly in parking areas. So, carry a good map and take time to collect the tourist brochures. These can be obtained from the Turistbyrås or Tourist Offices which are found in all the larger towns and, indeed, in any area popular with visitors. Apart from handing out a great quantity of literature (it is rare to find a brochure which is not translated into English) the Tourist Offices give help in booking hotel accommodation and rail, coach or ferry tickets. Visitors who want information in advance of their trip are likely to get most of what they need by writing to the Tourist Information Centre in Stockholm or by contacting the Tourist Secretary at a Swedish Embassy. In Britain, the Embassy address is: 23 North Row, London W1R 2DN. Free publications are available on winter sports, boat hire, hiking, budget price accommodation and just about every other topic of possible interest to the traveller, including a complete list of Tourist Information Offices, their addresses, telephone numbers and the times of opening and closing. A complete guide to camp sites in Sweden, for both tents and caravans is published by the Riksorganisationernas Camping Kommitté, Kungsgatan 34 IV, 111 35 Stockholm. Called simply *The Camping Book*, it costs 10 kronor or just over one pound. Once armed with essential guide material there is no need to worry about obtaining special permission to embark on this or that area of exploration. Everyone shares the ancient legal right to wander freely or pitch a tent in fields (except cultivated land), woods or on beaches. The custom of Allemansrätt or 'every man's rights' dates from the period when roads were so few and far between that almost any journey involved crossing private land. Now it is regarded as a freeman's charter to protect the interests of all those who enjoy the outdoor life. 'Trespassers will be Prosecuted' is not a sign you are ever likely to see in Sweden.

The choice of accommodation ranges from the five-star city hotel to the private house in the country offering Rum att Hyra. Taken in isolation this statement implies nothing exceptional but what is unusual about Sweden is that whatever the price, standards are never less than tolerable. There is thus some purpose in looking at what is an offer in the smaller hotels or hostels which might otherwise be ignored until the holiday money starts running out. One of the unlikeliest organisations in the hotel business is the Salvation Army. What were homes for the destitute until social welfare robbed them of their function have been converted into commercial operations providing clean and comfortable rooms at moderate prices. Also reliable are the YMCA and YWCA (youth hostels often have family rooms), the Swedish National Traffic Association (STTF) the Swedish Touring Club (STF) and the Society for the Promotion of Skiing and Open Air Life (SkiF). The last two are particularly helpful to those trying to find the top of the country. They have opened hotels in Lapland which are as good as anything in the middle-range accommodation available in the peak tourist areas. They also administer mountain cabins which can be hired for a small fee for overnight stops.

The one thing you cannot rely on in a Swedish hotel is a great deal of personal service. With high labour costs, employing a man to carry bags involves an increase in prices which is out of all proportion to the real value of his work. So, you take your own luggage to your room. Similarly, if there are shoes to be cleaned, drinks to be ordered and newspapers to be collected you can be quite sure who will end up doing all the lifting and carrying. Rising labour costs are also responsible for recent big increases in the price of restaurant meals. To eat economically in Sweden is to choose self-service. Fortunately, this can be a cheerfully satisfying experience because most self-service restaurants try hard to maintain reasonable standards.

Several stages on from the help-yourself meals, is to eat at

one of the increasing number of road houses known as
Värdshus or Gästgivargårdar. These are the closest the
Swedes get to the British inn. They are generally cosy and
friendly with a menu that includes the regional specialities.
But don't expect to feed on the cheap. Prices are about the
same or even higher than those in a good-class restaurant
anywhere else in Europe. And don't bother asking for dishes
that are not a regular part of the national diet. Apart from a
few standard French and Italian recipes, foreign cuisine is as
yet a rare experience in Sweden. Even in Stockholm the
overwhelming majority of good and very good restaurants are
Swedish-owned with Swedish chefs preparing traditional
Swedish meals.

7. Gothenburg or Göteborg

Whatever the choice of travel, air or sea, the chances are that an introduction to Sweden will be via the first or second city of the country – Stockholm or Gothenburg. Both are long-established as busy trade centres with good access to the international trade routes but Stockholm, though basically a city built on islands, is in fact several miles from what might properly be described as the coastline while Gothenburg harbour, at the mouth of the River Göta, is in sight of the open sea. There are other points of contrast but to avoid jumping back and forth, the toss of a coin has decided that the tour starts in Gothenburg.

First time visitors to Gothenburg (or Göteborg to give the proper Swedish name) are often tempted to bypass the city with a few complimentary phrases about its commercial and trading prowess. All those habour cranes dipping and delving in some slow-motion ritual for the consumer society, the noise and smell of industry, the sober office blocks – surely a place for business men not for tourists. It is true that commerce has the first claim on the city. One third of Sweden's imports and a quarter of her exports go through Gothenburg. But quite apart from the multitude of trading services, there is a big shipbuilding industry, which has a thing or two to teach the rest of the world about the science of automation and its effect on productivity, the Volvo headquarters and SKF not to mention a thriving textile industry centred a few miles out of Borås. But these are relative newcomers to the Gothenburg scene which has a cultural tradition going way back beyond the advent of the technological revolution. Perhaps for this reason the city seems to have a life of its own, taking support from its industry but, as has happened so often elsewhere, being overwhelmed and absorbed by it.

The people are proudly independent and are quite unable to understand how anyone could think of good reasons for living in some other city. Local politicians who progress to national responsibilities and artists who stay away from home too long are looked upon with great suspicion. 'Why should they want to leave?' ask the loyalists in a tone of pained surprise. After, all, Gothenburg has its own political and cultural environment not to mention a fine university and many top-grade specialist educational institutes – surely scope enough to satisfy all reasonable aspirations.

The city was founded at the beginning of the seventeenth century when Sweden's choice of outlet to the sea was limited by the fact that most of the Western coastline was controlled by the Danes. Notable landmarks still are two of the forts built at that time – Kronan (the Crown) and Lejonet (the Lion). In the early days the settlement chiefly benefited the traders of the Dutch East India Company whose influence was such that they held a clear majority on the municipal council and conducted all important business in their native tongue. But this preliminary chapter was abruptly concluded by a Danish invasion and almost total destruction of the town. The rebuilding of Gothenburg was one of the achievements of Gustavus Adolphus, Sweden's great warrior king, and with the emergence of Sweden as a European power, it quickly expanded to become Stockholm's closest rival as a centre for political and economic power.

Foreign influence remained strong but now broadened to take in Germans and Scots, the latter mostly in search of a friendly refuge from English persecution. But it seems that even here they were reminded of past battles since English immigrants were also much in evidence. Indeed, the man who created Gustavus' powerful battle fleet, Frederick Chapman, was the son of an Englishman who had settled in Gothenburg.

In practice, the English and Scots were more than tolerably

pleasant to each other, even co-operating in the setting up of the Swedish East India Company which for about half a century maintained a thriving trade. The only part of the Company still in evidence is the premises which are now used to house the exhibits of the Museum of Ethnography. With the continuing growth of western trade and cultural links, later generations dubbed the city Little London, a title which today's Gothenburgers might dismiss as just a trifle patronising but which still serves as a reminder of their cosmopolitan tradition.

To explore Gothenburg is to enjoy a feeling of spaciousness. Largely rebuilt after a huge fire in 1800, the city was opened up to accommodate a cluster of parks and gardens and broad tree-lined avenues. Even in the narrower streets of the Old Town there is no feeling of overcrowding since the latest policy is to create traffic-free shopping precincts with patches of flowers where there used to be parking bays. An immediate impression – but a personal one which others may not appreciate so enthusiastically – is that Gothenburg has had the good civic sense to maintain an efficient and economic tramway system. But even if the characteristic lurch and clatter of the trams are unappealing, there is no question that public transport is reliable and traffic kept to manageable proportions. Another snap opinion which is more likely to win general acceptance is that the fish restaurants are marvellous. And so they should be since Gothenburg is Scandinavia's largest fishing port. Anyone wanting confirmation of the fact should visit the early-morning fish auctions where a careless flick of the eyelid or a brisk wave can put one into the trade in a very big way.

To enjoy the 'fruits from the sea' try three of the restaurants recommended by Gothenburgers – Fiskekrogen in the city centre, Långedrag, which is on the coast a short distance outside the city, and Henriksberg, which is more expensive but has a good view of the harbour.

The centre of Gothenburg is also the oldest district and is part of the inheritance from the seventeenth-century Dutch traders. Now a lively shopping area it claims to offer the best in fashion and design. All the famous Swedish departmental stores – NK, Ahléns, IKEA – are in or close to the Old Town while unique to Gothenburg is the famous Ferdinand Lundquist store. The pleasure of wandering through these shops does not depend on the capacity to spend vast sums. The special displays and general presentation, particularly of furniture, add up to an adventure in aesthetics, which is well worth experiencing for its own sake. The best of the craft shops are grouped together in what was, in the seventeenth century, the Kronhuset or Crown House but is now referred to as Krononhusbodarna. One of the delights of this building is that it provides comfortable facilities for a rest and snack before embarking on the next stage of the sightseeing expedition.

It is easy enough to spot the Old Town on the map because it is bounded by a waterway, another survival from the Dutch occupation. This is a convenient reminder to take a boat trip along what remains of the old canal network (not quite so impressive as the brochures suggest since it is really only a single canal which happens to go round in a circle) and out into the harbour for a closer view of the crowded waterfront. A more ambitious boating expedition leads under the Álvsborgsbron Bridge with its one-kilometre span of the harbour, to the mouth of the River Göta and the island fortress of Älvsborg. Once the forward defence post for Gothenburg and the centre piece for great naval battles, and later a prison, Elfsborg has finally surrendered to the mass army of tourists. The tiny eighteenth-century church is much in demand for weddings.

Back to the Old Town for the start of a leisurely walk up Kungsportsavenyn – more usually known simply as Avenyn or the Avenue – a long boulevard which melds heavy early-century architecture with higher but more impersonal modern blocks. (Will visitors in fifty or a hundred years' time find more definite signs of character in our designs for living?). At the very top is Götaplatsen, the cultural centre of

Gothenburg, boozed by a twin-staged theatre, concert hall (home of the Gothenburg Symphony Orchestra), art museum and library. From whatever direction you arrive it is really quite impossible to miss the place since slap in the middle of the square is the gigantic Milles fountain sculpture of the sea god Poseidon.

What can be said of Carl Milles? Certainly he is much revered in Sweden. Almost every large town regards it as a matter of prestige that at least one item of his work should be on permanent show. But some modern critics, looking perhaps for art with a social message, think of him as rather passé. A more popular reaction is that his sculptures are at least compelling if not aways endearing. This is doubtless true of Poseidon whose recognisable human links (with one central feature curiously out of scale) are surmounted by a grotesque head. But resist an instant verdict in favour of seeing more of the Milles output in the art museum, which also contains examples of other Swedish masters such as Anders Zorn, Carl Larson, Ernst Josephson (his Water Sprite is instantly recognisable), and Carl Hill.

The sheer scope of interest of the rest of Gothenburg's museums and exhibitions is impressive by the standards of any large city. The problem for the guide is to know where to start and where to finish. A visit to the Maritime Museum is recommended if only to see the collection of ship models – large, small, minuscule, of every age and category – which must be unrivalled. A few steps away from the Museum is the Sailors' Monument, a statue of a woman staring longingly out to sea. She is said to represent the spirit of the great nautical adventure and is solemnly respected in Gothenburg but cynics have been heard to claim that she might more accurately reflect the seaman's philosophy of life if she were seen shaking her fist.

The Museum of National Antiquities re-creates the story of the art and craft movement in the west of Sweden and is particularly notable for its fine collection of tapestries. It shares with several other Swedish museums the virtue of not being afraid to exhibit contemporary objects so that the visitor can easily understand the logic of continuing and developing tradition. Another museum with much to offer in the way of appreciating Swedish art and craft is Röhsaka Konstslöjdmuseet which concentrates on displaying items from the home – furniture, pottery, glass and the vast array of ornaments which have survived the test of changing tastes and the annual spring cleaning.

Natural history is well represented with a geological and zoological collection displayed at Slottskogen or the Castle Wood. This is one of the several large public parks in Gothenburg, each of which caters for one or more special interests. Apart from its Museum of Natural History, Slottskogen has a stadium and a zoo; Trädgardsföreningen or the Garden Society, close to the city centre, maintains a permanent show of tropical plants; and the Bantaniska Trädgården or Botanical Gardens has just about everything but is particularly proud of a rock garden which contains over 3,000 species of European, Asiatic and American plants. To shift into a lighter mood, the big amusement centre in Gothenburg is known as Liseberg. It has a variety theatre, concert hall, five dance halls and wide choice of restaurants, all in a park setting. On summer evenings most of the city, natives and visitors, seems to gather there.

Gothenburg is almost dead centre of a line of tourist resorts stretching along the coast from the Norwegian border in the north to the ferry links with Denmark in the south. This side of the country has always found special favour with holiday makers because the Gulf Stream creates a welcome boost to summer temperatures and the landscape or, perhaps, more particularly the seascape, is sufficiently varied to satisfy the needs of a broad cross-section of visitors. In general terms the Bohuslän region to the north of Gothenburg has a rocky shoreline with smooth tightly padded boulders like solidified bubbles while the southern Halland region has exclusive claim to the long sandy beaches. The provinces vie with each other for special credits. The Halland resorts emphasise their appeal to young families and imply that the facilities of their northern rivals are best suited to needs of trainee mountainers. The reply from Bohuslän is the promise of better fishing and sailing, and the claim that, anyway, the whole business of seaside holidays in Sweden started in Strömstad at the northernmost point of the west coast, where bathing was fashionable as early as the 1790s.

It is impossible to make a dogmatic judgment on these relative merits but it is fair to point out that for the foreign visitor there may not be much that is unexpected about a stretch of sand, however warm and silver, whereas the granite grey rock in all its fantastic shapes and sizes, whether on the coast by the lakes or in the countryside, is more closely associated with the unique beauty of the Swedish scene than any other single feature, not excepting the great pine forests. The sheer grandeur of the rock formations can be best appreciated if the view is taken from the water – and there are so many boat owners in Sweden it is most improbable that anyone leaves without this opportunity. This is a theme that will recur later in the journey and I will not labour the point here except to say that Gothenburg itself has a fabulous archipelago and that much of the west coast is scattered with fjords and islands.

Using Gothenburg as a base, there are great possibilities for one- or two-day coastal cruises. To the north are the bathing and fishing resorts of Uddevalla, Lysekil, Smögen and Strömstad and the island town of Marstrand which is famous for its sailing community and their big event – the annual regatta. Southwards, there is Laholm, a cosy old town which used to attract fishermen until industrial pollution drove away the salmon but still does attract artists who find it a congenial spot to live. At nearby Båstad, international golf and tennis tournaments are held throughout the summer.

Varberg is one of the many coastal towns which can boast a castle but there is something exceptional about this one. It accommodates fourteenth-century man, a perfectly preserved fully clothed body which was excavated from an area of marshland. This unfortunate character, who was murdered and staked to the ground, apparently to stop him haunting his killers, now serves as one of the few reliably accurate representations of what people wore in the medieval period.

Falkenberg is another popular bathing resort but also attracts tourists to its Törngren Pottery which has been in the same family since the eighteenth century. At Halmstead there is a mini-Sweden consisting of hundreds of models of well-known buildings. If the idea of sea travel is unappealing, at least visit the islands of Orust and Tjörn via the three Tjörn bridges which connect with the mainland at Stenungsund. They are in the right place and at the right height to serve as observation points for a panoramic slice of granite-studded coastline.

To change the perspective, the landward side of the west coast offers much in the way of archaeological and historical interest. That the area was relatively congenial even in prehistoric times is suggested by the number of places that boast rock carvings and burial mounds from the Bronze and Iron Ages. Viking settlements are also in evidence and at Blomsholm, just a few miles from Strömstad, a ship burial has been excavated.

At a later period, with much of the west coast disputed territory among the Scandinavians, the military was frequently at work and castle and fortress building was almost a local industry. Many of these survived – the fourteenth-century Bohus Fortress at Kungälv for instance, and the early seventeenth-century Carlsten Fortress at Marstrand. To the south, Varberg's fortress has a 700-year pedigree and the Halmstead stronghold is sixteenth-century. Tjolöholm likes to claim that it has its own castle but it is more a large country house and though Tudor in style was, in fact, built in the nineteenth century – a mere youngster dressed up as an adult – though nonetheless quite imposing.

Travelling the west coast without detecting the sense of history is not impossible, but what is totally inescapable is the evidence of the social and economic influence of a single

9 Stortorget, the central square of Malmö.

occupation. The fishing industry is still king – even though there are signs of failing energy as industrialisation saps up land and labour. Nowadays fewer boats set out and an increasing proportion of those still in the business cater mostly for the tourist anglers. But the region to the north is scattered with tiny fishing villages, their red, wooden houses crowding the water's edge.

Thoughts of the sea brings us back to the ever interesting topic of sea-food meals. A chapter could be filled with recommendations to visit this or that restaurant but shortening the list to very special favourites start with a ferry ride from Hovenäset near Kungshamn to an island called Bohus Malmön and the restaurant Draget. The place doesn't look very impressive, being a converted co-op shop, but it has a magnificent view of the entire coastline and the food is excellent. Another popular restaurant is Tanums Hede Gästqivaregård, an old inn built in 1620, within easy reach of the E6, Strömstad and Uddevalla. If you feel like extending the menu to take in meat dishes try Mahults Herrgårds Pensionat or Mahult's Inn near Halmstad which is an attractive yellow wooden house close to the lake. The speciality is lambsteak and the distinguishing feature of the meal, apart from the quality of the cooking, is the facility for taking coffee in the garden at the same time as watching the boats pull in at the quayside.

10 Kalmar Castle.

8. The Göta Canal to Lake Vättern

If, as cruising devotees insist, a boat journey is a relaxing experience, then the effect of travelling by waterway from Gothenburg across central Sweden is positively soporific. It takes three days by steamer to cover the 300-mile trip up the Göta River, across Vänern (Sweden's largest lake and the second largest in Europe) through the Göta Canal, over Lake Vättern and then back on to the canal to Lake Roxen and the coastal town of Oxelösund. The boat finds its way inland again via the Södertälje Canal and Lake Mälaren which links directly with Stockholm.

The credit for opening up this extraordinary cross-country route belongs to the engineer, politician and industrialist, Baltzar van Platen, who spent twenty years raising support and finance for his Göta Canal project. The concept, involving the construction of about 60 miles of artificial waterway was more remarkable than might at first appear since the levels vary as much as 300 feet and at several points the steamer must negotiate complicated lock systems. Van Platen died in 1829, three years before the Göta Canal was completed. Perhaps if he had lived, the project would have disappointed him since its commercial viability was soon to be threatened by railways. For most of its history the water route has appealed chiefly to passengers who can afford the time and, latterly, the cost of a leisurely excursion.

Because the size of the boats is determined by the narrowest point on the waterway, they are unable to achieve the economies of carrying a large compliment of passengers. Thus, all-the-way tickets are very expensive – even by Swedish standards. The cost of a single cabin on the bridge deck with all meals can be as much as £100. Savings on the budget and on the holiday schedule can be achieved by signing on for only part of the trip. But which part? The visitor might feel as if he is buying a picture without first seeing what is in the gallery. Everyone has their favourite view but the value of personal recommendation is limited by the embarrassing fact that few of us who write so boldly of the sights and pleasures of Sweden have actually experienced the entire journey. Since I am one of those whose research, at least in this respect, is undeniably incomplete, the best I can do is, first, to chat about places which can be appreciated as easily from the landward side as from the water and then to pass the reader on to Birgitta Ahlberg, whose book *A trip on the Göta Canal* has been translated into English. Hopefully, a more recently published volume *Göta Kanal – handbook för en lustresa* by Jan Gabrielson will soon appear in an international edition.

The province that is best served by the Göta route is Västergötland. Flanked on one side by the Göta River and Lake Vänern and on the other by Lake Vättern, the two are linked by a stretch of canal which bisects the northern end of the region.

The land here is almost perfectly flat and the Göta canal is seldom visible to anyone who is not standing close to the edge. When I was in the area for the first time, visiting a friend's country home, the first knowledge I had that we were close to the canal was the startling realisation that a steamer was gliding past the bottom of the garden. If watching the boats pass by is your pleasure (and a very restful pastime it can be) and you don't happen to meet any local farmers offering a private view, spend some time at the delightful Kanalhotellet which is just a few yards from the water at Karlsborg. This establishment, which has catered for canal gazers since the beginning of the century, offers a bonus attraction of a restaurant serving fresh red trout from Lake Vättern. Karlsborg , incidentally, boasts an impressive monument to the futility of military planning – a virtually impregnable fortress which took nearly a century to build and was completed just in time for the experience of the First World War to prove that such defences were totally obsolete. To the north and extending into Närke, Sweden's smallest province, is a wild forest region known as Tiveden. Once a handy refuge for outlaws it is now a nature reserve much loved by the category of hikers who favour strenuous activity and possess a good sense of direction. The lakes, formed in the hollows of Ice Age rocks, are distinguished in summer by a red glow created by one of Nature's rarities – rose-coloured water lilies.

To return to the Göta Canal, the rural seclusion of this part of Västergötland contrasts greatly with the scene on the first leg of the journey. The banks of the Göta River are heavily industrialised and the first series of locks, at Trollhättan, are massive automatically operated structures accommodating ocean-going vessels, while those after Lake Vänern are small and shallow and require a lock-keeper to operate the mechanism by sheer muscle-power. The history of the Trollhättan locks date back to 1800 when the short stretch of canal of which they are a part connected Lake Vänern with the navigable section of the Göta River and opened up the water route to Gothenburg. It was quite an achievement for the time since the locks had to be steeply banked to bypass a series of spectacular waterfalls. Sadly, all that is now left of what was one of the favourite tourist sights in Sweden is a deep and dry gorge. The water is held back for a hydro-electric project which powers most of southern Sweden. It is difficult imagining today's environmentalist lobby even allowing such a scheme to leave the drawing board but Trollhättan has at least served as a powerful argument against the careless exploitation of water resources elsewhere in the country.

Entering Lake Vättern the canal steamers edge south to take in a visit to Vadstena, a medieval town which has somehow escaped the recent and now frequently regretted Swedish passion for all things modern. Vadstena has been twice blessed, first by St Bridget who founded the Abbey round which the town developed and latterly by the Göta Canal Company which has rescued the district from obscurity and economic decline by bringing in the tourists.

There is a lot of affection for St Bridget even from those who are otherwise unmoved by Christianity. She was born at the beginning of the fourteenth cntury, married at the age of thirteen and had eight children. The next big event in her life came in 1344 after the death of her husband. She had a vision of Christ which she interpreted as an invitation to build a monastery and to recruit men and women for a new religious order. She initiated the enterprise by persuading the King to grant her an estate at Vadstena. But royal favour proved vacillatory and she decided that what she really needed was a Papal blessing. So, she set off first to Avignon where the Pope was spending a self-imposed exile and then later to Rome to continue her pleading for acknowledgment and support. The great quality of St Bridget was her refusal to accept defeat. It took years of tireless effort, or as some might say, maniacal devotion, and the death of one Pope before she was given permission to set up an order at Vadstena. By way of thanksgiving she promptly set off with two of her children on a pilgrimage to the Holy Land, a journey which prevented her ever returning to Sweden for she died soon after her return to Rome. Meanwhile, a small community, having established itself at Vadstena, now grew rapidly while Bridget's daughter stayed on in Rome to pressurise for her mother's canonisation, a task in which she succeeded in 1391.

The St Bridget Abbey still accommodates a thriving religious community and provides more or less continuous hospitality for those who used to be called pilgrims and nowadays are more often known as delegates to ecclesiastical conferences. Along the shore, various medieval and Renaissance buildings, including the oldest court house in the country, attract interest but attention inevitably focuses on the moated Castle. It is a heavyweight edifice built in the mid sixteenth century by Gustav Vasa, Sweden's first uncompromisingly nationalistic leader who freed the country from Danish rule. The castle has survived a violent history without any immediately noticeable signs of wear and tear. Ironically it came closest to ruin when it was abandoned by the military. Between 1750 and 1870 it was used as a granary, its treasures having been transferred to the palaces at Gripsholm and Drottningholm. The Abbey was similarly ransacked of its great library which was split between Uppsala University and the Royal Library in Stockholm. Nonetheless, Vadstena looks very well without the embellishments – a credit to ancient crafts and modern restoration.

A little way up the coast and also on the visiting list of the Göta steamer is a small and modern town called Motala. The headquarters of the Canal Company is situated here, approximately enough since its instigators, Baltzar van Platen, lived nearby. He founded a still prospering engineering business, Motala Verkstad, which takes credit for building Sweden's first screw-vessel and her first railway engine. Just inland from Motala, on a bank of the Canal is the grave of von Platen, a marble mausoleum with steps leading down to the water. Having pointed out the monument, a convenient excuse is needed to leave the Göta Canal because I like to think of the steamer acknowledging their maker with a reverential toot and, in this instance, I have no wish to be disillusioned by reality. But in fact, there is practical reason for changing routes. This is an easy jumping on point for a roundabout tour of Lake Vättern – following the tarmac perimeter. On the map it looks as if the planners have boobed again, taking the road far too close to the shoreline. But, in practice they have performed a very creditable job of bringing the motorist in close to the favoured camping and picnic spots while somehow not allowing the traffic to dominate the scene. Possibly the secret is in having a low traffic density, for even on the E4 – the intercontinental motorway which touches the east side of Lake Vättern from Ödeshög to Huskvarna – there is seldom any overcrowding. This is just as well because the views over the water can be perilously diverting for a driver who has to keep one eye on the juggernauts.

I always think of this area as on the way to or from somewhere since most Swedes seem to know it as a weekend or overnight stop. Certainly there are many quiet and pleasant little towns not far from the main route which derive a healthy income from reviving the energy and spirits of long-distance travellers. The top favourite is Gränna, a one-street community on the edge of the lake, known for its old-world charm, its new-world ability to cater for the summer influx of tourists without panic or fuss and the manufacture of peppermint rock which has been a local industry since the eighteenth century. The Gränna hotels are likely to be booked in advance but there is really no general shortage of accommodation in the neighbourhood. I once discovered a stately home that had been converted into a hotel by the simple process of hiring a few part-time staff and fixing a bed-and-breakfast sign to the main gate. While this can't be good news for the Swedish aristocrats, who have little enough to be pleased about, I must say that I welcomed the homely touch even if I did have to sleep under the accusing gaze of the family portraits. The name of the hotel in Västanå Gård. While it has nothing to offer in the way of sustenance except breakfast, there is just down the road the excellent Gyllene Uttern or Golden Otter Hotel, a more expensive but heavily booked hotel which has a baronial-style restaurant overlooking the lake.

For those who prefer their domestic comforts to be moulded in plastic there are plenty of ultra-modern motels. And, to return to the earlier point that the district caters particularly well for people in a hurry, I should add that the Gyllene Uttern advertises not only a fine restaurant and overnight chalets on a high ridge facing the lake and the island of Visingö but also its own wedding chapel.

Continuing down the E4 towards Malmö is to enter the province of Skåne, and flat, rich, farm country of a quality that is unknown in the rest of Sweden. That the country is almost self-sufficient in basic foodstuffs is largely a tribute to the productivity of Skåne agriculture since less than ten per cent of Sweden's land surface is suitable for arable crops. The whole business of modern farming in Sweden started here in the late eighteenth century when the region was already noted for its potential as 'the perfect breadbasket' for the nation. A landowner with the unlikely name of Baron Rutger Maclean, followed a visit to England with the decision to impose on his own tenants ideas he had picked up on new methods of husbandry. Small and scattered family-controlled parcels of land were merged into compact and more easily manageable units. But he departed from the English pattern by disbanding the village communities (in some cases literally blowing up the houses) in favour of isolated homesteads, a policy soon approved by the government and adopted by other landowners. The administrative and social changes increased efficiency but by destroying the traditional pattern of village life they created a need among farming people to belong – to feel part of a community. Hence the emergence of the popular movements – religious and political – which have had and in many cases still do have such a powerful influence on social attitudes. The village idea has never been reinstated and the contemporary traveller's impression of Skåne is of a generously fertile spread of land studded by tiny settlements of farm buildings.

The big food companies like Findus have taken over the commercial leadership of the region and for the most part the power of the independent landowners is just a memory contained within the surviving manor houses and castles. There are well over 200 of these noble houses in Skåne, all carefully preserved and many open to the public, including Baron Maclean's home, Svaneholm Castle, between Svedala and Skurup. As a fitting memorial to the great man, several of the largest rooms in the Castle – the knights' hall, the hall room and the cellar – have been converted into restaurants. Svaneholm is just the place to sample the traditional Skåne goose dinner and its equally traditional starter – the notorious blood soup. One other point about Svaneholm. Its history did not begin and end with the achievement of Baron Maclean. Its origins are in the sixteenth century when its owner was Elizabeth Trolle. She came into possession of the place as a result of her husband's efforts to think of an original twist to the old custom of exchanging gifts the morning after the wedding night. When Elizabeth woke up, Svaneholm Castle was hers.

The other great houses of Skåne range the chronological scale. Bosjökloster Castle, at one time a Benedictine monastery, is 900 years old, Glimmingehus is the best-preserved medieval castle in Scandinavia, Christinehof is a fine example of eighteenth-century construction, while at Backåkra, on the south-east tip of Skåne, Dag Hammarskjöld's farm attracts large numbers of visitors. Sofiero, once a royal summer residence well-known for its carefully tended garden displays, was given to the people of Hälsingsborg in 1974, after the death of the old king.

A visit to one of the great houses should allow time for exploring the nearby churches distinguished by their roofs which in cross-section look like twin staircases. The unassuming simplicity of their design, invariably emphasised by whitewashed walls, suggests they are at their best when observed as part of the broad landscape. But likely enough the reward for pausing for a moment to look inside is to discover the vivid imagery of early religious belief, expressed in the language of wall paintings. In a sense these pictorial stories with their harsh biblical messages signify a rebirth of medieval art, since in many cases the pictures were blotted out by later generations and only lately have resurfaced from under layers of dull domestic paint. The wonder of restoration, achieved by the same painstaking effort as went into the original creation, is as much emphasised by what is missing as by what has been saved – the ragged edges where the colours fade into the plaster or the abrupt interruption in a storey where the stone has been removed to allow for more window space. How much else could have happened to wipe out all traces of medieval worship?

The people of Skåne are more extrovert than other Swedes

and, being so, are only too happy to point out other ethnographical characteristics which distinguish them from the rest of their countrymen. Enjoying good food and having plenty of it on their doorstep they are less inclined to join in the fashionable pursuit of the slender waist. They are known for their capacity for fun and easy-going conviviality which seems to be more in tune with the Danish way of life. The association is not very surprising since Skåne has close geographical and historical links with that country. As late as the mid-seventeenth century the province was actually part of the Danish kingdom and after it was taken by Sweden in 1658, the old loyalties and sympathies remained strong. Today, the cultural mix is best observed in the coastal towns. In particular, Hälsningborg, which is a brief ferry trip across the Sound from the Danish town of Helsingör or, if Shakespeare is the guide, Elsinore, successfully merges old and new architectural styles from both countries, with much respect given to the Danish preference for dominating the skyline with green copper roofs. One of the great sights of Hälsingborg is the night view of the Danish coastline along Sjaelland which, brightly illuminated over its entire length, is known as Queen Ingrid's Necklace. It is best seen from the top of Kärnan, a medieval tower which is the only surviving part of the old fortifications. The Danes have kept their defences in better shape. The green spires of Kronberg Castle, made famous as a scene stealer for Shakespeare's Hamlet, are clearly visible from the Swedish side.

Up the coast from Hälsingborg is Höganäs, an industrial town which has an old-established pottery business and quite a number of individually well-known potters. Further on towards the tip of the peninsula are Arild and Mölle, two quiet fishing villages which are popular with artists and writers. One of the hotels, in Mölle, Kullagårdens Värdshus, is comfortable in a homely sort of way and specialises in catering for those who enjoy long walks and rural splendours.

The capital of Skåne, and the South is Malmö. Sweden's third largest city and major port with its 2,700 acres of docks gets less attention that it deserves because tourists have their interest fixed on the excitements of Copenhagen, now brought within closer reach by a hydrofoil service which crosses the Sound between the two countries in a mere thirty-five minutes. Yet ignoring the ever-widening sprawl of self-consciously clean and bright and thoroughly modern building enterprises, the city is not without its attractions.

Just off centre is Malmöhus Castle, built by a Danish king when Malmö was the second city in Denmark. Now a museum the castle is surrounded by a fabulous leisure area of parkland, lakes and waterways. Inevitably, there are several Milles' sculptures to admire, including the famous Pegasus team of man and horse soaring through space. Outside the castle grounds there are a few reminders of Malmö's medieval antecedents. The green-roofed Town Hall (Rådhuset) on the big market square was built in 1546 and restyled in the nineteenth century, while, close by St Peter's Church can claim a nearer association with the genuine Renaissance design. But there is no getting away from the fact that Malmö is essentially a modern and highly prosperous industrial city with the strongest appeal for those who can enjoy the contemporary scene without hankering too much for the charm of history.

The big hotels' claim to top grading is justified by the standards of their restaurants. The restaurant in the Scandinavia Hotel is excellent and the Savoy superb but very expensive. It is no coincidence that the latter is the headquarters of the Swedish Gastronomical Society. But turn into any street in Malmö and you are likely to discover a good eating place. Among the more popular are Rådhuskällaren, a cellar restaurant in the Town Hall and Tunneln, also subterranean but more distinguished, being fourteenth-century and the oldest tavern in Scandinavia.

The city has a good theatre, built as they say, before its time and now, thirty years later still one of the biggest in Europe; sports enthusiasts can choose between Jägersro race trace and a new athletics stadium; and there are exhibitions galore with

Skånemässan, a commercial and industrial exhibition held towards the end of the summer, as the big international attraction.

Malmö is a good base from which to embark on a castle and church spotting journey through Skåne. The possible routes are innumerable and can safely be left to individual choice but a natural for the first stopping-off point is the university town of Lund, just ten miles away. This has been the great centre of learning since the middle ages and the quietly academic atmosphere of the town has been faithfully retained. The twelfth-century cathedral, a fine Romanesque structure with two massive square towers, was built at a time when Lund what the Christian focal point for all Scandinavia, a claim that could hardly be disputed when the city limit encompassed twenty-two churches and seven monasteries. An ideal time for visiting the Cathedral is around noon for it is then that the mechanical wizardry of the Middle Ages is on display. One of those clocks which tell you everything from the time of day to the position of the stars, acknowledges the midday hour with an organ melody and a short divinity lesson enacted by the three wise men who pop out of their cubicles in the clock face to file past the Virgin and Child. The founder of Lund, incidentally, is said to have been King Canute who named his city after London, the centre of his English dominion.

A short drive south from Malmö is the tiny community of Hvellinge and its restaurant Hvellinge Gästgivargård , made famous by the annual gathering of Nobel prizewinners who come here after receiving their awards for a celebratory Christmas dinner. If these surroundings are too august for a relaxing meal keep driving a few miles to Skivarp, another small village with another famous restaurant, Skivarps Gästgiveri. The great virtue of this establishment is that you can choose either traditional Skåne food or more exotic continental dishes or even Chinese and Indonesian specialities. An after-lunch drive further along the coast brings you to Ystad, a medieval town that lends itself to slow wandering. There is a broad sandy beach highly recommended by sea and sun bathers. But leave time in the day for one last call, to Svenstorp, where lives the artist craftsman Gösta Israelsson. He makes bowls – beech bowls, pine bowls, birch bowls, even bowls from the wood of fruit trees. They are without question the most extraordinary bowls you have ever seen – gently shaped, multi-shaded and gorgeously smooth objects, which epitomise the Swedish ideal of utilitarian creativity.

9. The South-east

Moving south out of Skåne and farming country is to find a more typically Swedish landscape – the rock and forest of Småland. If asked to select their best personal qualities the people will tell you they are tough and inventive – they must be to make a living, quite unlike those pampered farmers of the south who have it all on a plate. The farmers of Skåne deny this, of course, and say that the Smålanders are just too mean to live well. It is true that extreme poverty is now only a memory shared by the older generation but there is still talk of the mass exodus in the late nineteenth century when, of the million or so emigrants who departed for the United States, over a third were escaping from the miserable little homesteads and depressed domestic industries of Småland. Their story is told vividly and movingly in Wilhelm Moberg's internationally famous series of books, *The Immigrants*.

Perhaps the sense of history is strong because modern industry in the province, though prospering, mostly remains tied to the ancient crafts and skills, practised in the same small local businesses which traditionally are the first to suffer from economic fluctuation. The notable example is the manufacture of glassware. This industry, which has contributed greatly to the reputation of Swedish design, is concentrated exclusively in Småland, indeed within a ten-mile radius of Växjö where over thirty glass companies, employing about 4,000 workers, are situated. Their agreed purpose is to create original and distinctive items of decorative glass. These can range from a piece of sculpture sold in a limited edition to wealthy collectors, to sets of wine glasses retailed by the big departmental stores. But whatever the finished article the quality of individuality is guaranteed because the manufacturing process is governed entirely by the talents of artists and craftsmen. Technology is permitted a look-in, only in so far as it can be an aid to individual skills – if, at any time, it is allowed to become a determinant for work performance then mass production and loss of identity must follow and that is a horror no-one in the glass industry cares to contemplate.

To see how the idea makes out in practice call at one of the glass works – Kosta, Boda and Orrefors are best-known and very popular with tourists but there are at least fifteen factories which welcome visitors. It is a commonplace to say of a difficult task that it can be made to look easy when performed by those with the right experience and training. But the thought is unlikely to be applied to this occupation for, however skilled the practitioner, it is impossible for the observer to forget that what is blown, rolled and shaped in such effortless style is a dollop of molten glass which comes out of the kiln at a temperature of 1200° centigrade. And the tools of the trade are not so much simple as primitive – blowpipe, wood-jack, block and mould – the same tools that have served the industry for hundreds of years. The blowpipe is an iron tube about a yard long. The glassblower dips the pipe into the molten glass and gives a quick twist to pick up just the right quantity. He uses his blowing power – sparingly – while the glass slowly takes shape in the mould. He is helped by others in the team – possibly six or seven specialists who perform such functions as fixing the stem or base to a goblet or cooling the glass. The work is carried out in a large shed which has the feel and look of an old-fashioned iron foundry – waves of heat from open furnaces tended by men in leather aprons who keep up a steady rhythm of activity, matching each other's movements so that no-one is ever unoccupied for more than a few seconds. Then it is the turn of the engraver. His equipment is more sophisticated but requires no less skill to operate. Fast-rotating copper discs cutting into the glass reproduce the artist's paper sketches. Not surprisingly, two years' training is required to become a skilled glassworker, and there is only one glass school – in Orrefors – which allows a few places to foreign students and also provides short courses for designers.

Most of the factories exhibit their finished articles and, to set the contemporary fashions in their historical context, in Växjö there is a museum collection which traces the development of glass-making from Roman times to the present. The appeal of handmade glass to visitors and to buyers all over Europe and the United States is undeniable, but costs are high – simply because the industry is labour-intensive – and there is much talk of achieving economies to keep prices steady. Increased mechanisation is opposed for the reasons given earlier, though in one or two cases a fair compromise has been reached between the technologists and the pure artists. For instance, at the Kosta glassworks, which turns out a range of table plates and dishes, a labour-saving pressing technique is employed but there are still craftsmen on hand who make minute changes to the amount of glass used in each pressing so that every piece is slightly different from the next.

By insisting on preserving craft practices, some of the smaller firms have forced themselves out of business or have merged with larger units while the survivors have narrowed their range to concentrate on the safely profitable lines. This rationalisation process, though generally accepted as inevitable, has brought complaints from the designers who anticipate less freedom to experiment with forms and materials. It may happen, but with designers like Erik Höglund who creates a remarkable three-dimensional effect with his glass sculptures; Signe Perrson-Melin who has developed a superbly attractive and eminently practical range of kitchen utensils which combine glass with stone and wood; and Bertil Valien who is probably the most adventurous mixer of colours and shapes, there is no immediate signs that inventiveness is being sacrified to conformity.

Talk of commercial rationalisation inevitably revives

11 The medieval ruins of Visby on the island of Gotland.

memories of what happened not so many years ago to a Småland industry which broke all records in market growth. In the 1920s, the Swedish Match Company, at Jönköping on the southern tip of Lake Vättern, was used as the base for the construction of a vast international business empire. The financial wizard responsible for this achievement was Ivar Kreuger who, having established his ascendancy in the Swedish economy, went on to negotiate multi-million-dollar loans to foreign governments in return for local match monopolies. Unfortunately the backing for these deals was less than substantial. It was an impressive juggling performance while it lasted but when one ball fell to the ground the entire act went to pieces. Kreuger committed suicide in 1932 shortly after one of his admirers, a prominent economist, had publicly expressed his regrets that the world had no statesmen of his calibre. Nowadays the match industry is administered less ambitiously but more successfully. There are no monuments to Kreuger to be seen in Jönköping, but the history of all other aspects of the business is on record in the museum which contains the largest collection of matchbox labels in the world.

The closest provincial rival of Jönköping as an industrial centre is Kalmar, a city of about 50,000 sited on the south-east coast facing the islands of Gotland and Öland. But if historical significance is any criterion for priority then Kalmar is way out in the lead. It was a prosperous trading community in the early Middle Ages, when foreign merchants, mostly from northern Germany, used it as a base for supplying the Scandinavian market. At the same time, Kalmar had great strategic importance since, in a period of localised wars, raiders were able to plan their attack to make use of Gotland and Öland as stepping stones to their main objective.

While Kalmar was experiencing growing pains, the country as a whole was coming to terms with the idea of absolute monarchy. The transition from local autonomy to strong centralised authority was not easy with the nobility frequently in revolt to protect their privileges, wars between the Scandinavian countries to decide territorial rights and violent

12 An aerial view of Stockholm showing the Royal Palace (centre) and on the right the old Parliament House. At the bottom right of the picture is the Opera House.

inter-family rivalry to secure the accession. But from this vast confusion of claim and counter-claim emerged a dynastic ambition greater than anything previously envisaged in this part of the world – the unification, no less, of Sweden, Norway and Denmark. The prospect took shape in the late fourteenth century when, by chance, both Norway and Denmark shared the same head of state. In Norway, Queen Margaret acted for son Olaf while in Denmark she assumed power after the death of her father King Valdemar, in 1375. It soon occurred to the Swedish nobility, many of whom had rights and properties in the other countries, that it might be safer and even positively beneficial to join forces rather than risk isolation and the possibility of attack. King Albert of Sweden, who had attracted opposition for his land-grabbing policy and for his preference for handing out honours and jobs to his German friends, was sent packing and Margaret was duly proclaimed 'first lady of Sweden and her lawful mistress'. It was now up to her to nominate a king, which she did in 1396 when her great-nephew Erik of Pomerania who was already King of Norway was declared ruler of Denmark and Sweden. The coronation took place the following year in Kalmar – at that time the second city in Sweden – Stockholm having presumably lost favour because it had held out so long in support of the disgraced Albert.

For all practical purposes the Kalmar Union lasted only as long as Margaret was the dominant personality in Scandinavian politics. After her death in 1412, Erik was unable to hold the support of the nobles and one revolt followed another.

His successors were equally unfortunate and though each insurrection led to a patchwork compromise which stopped short at destroying the intent of the Kalmar Union, it was only a matter of time before a leader emerged who was capable of snatching independence for the Swedes. It was at the beginning of the sixteenth century when at last the break was made. The leader of the revolt, Gustav Vasa, who was elected King of Sweden in 1523, is one of the half dozen or so best-known figures in the country's history. He set the foundations for the modern Swedish state, promoted the Reformation and curbed the power of the nobility. Also, he spent a large part of the state income on building up a defence system which included, among other formidable bulwarks, a massive fortress and palace overlooking the Kalmar Sound. Thus, ironically, the man who finally destroyed the Kalmar Union, gave to that city something far more lasting.

The moated castle, one of the finest examples of its period in Europe, can still be seen today in the full glory of its extravagant Renaissance style. With its spires and round towers, it looks, as many observers have pointed out, like a fairty-tale castle. But once inside the grey walls the sheer might of the place is so overwhelming it can come as no surprise that it was once known as 'the lock and key of Sweden'.

Nowadays all the state rooms are open to visitors and are often used for public functions. The atmosphere on these occasions is historically authentic. Having spent an evening in the castle wining and dining with members of the town council I can vouch that it needs only a few glasses of Swedish schnapps to raise the thought that the walk back along the torchlit corridors is somethat risky for any gentleman not armed with a sword. Such revelries apart, Kalmar is a rather sedate city as befits its central architectural features which, dating mostly from the seventeenth century, are grand but sombre. The Italian Baroque Cathedral, for instance, was built between 1660 and 1700, the Court House, though influenced by the German Style, is roughly contemporary, and there are many town houses of the period.

If the search is for relics of an earlier historical setting it is necessary to extend the scope of investigation to Öland and Gotland. Nothing could be easier than the journey to the first of these islands because it is linked to the mainland by a new 3½-mile highway bridge – the longest in Europe. Interestingly, this costly enterprise which was intended to boost tourism has achieved too much, too quickly. When it opened in 1972 it was anticipated that less than a million cars a year would use the bridge. In fact it carried well over three million vehicles and further numbers are expected to be even higher. The fear, of course, is that Öland will be swamped by sightseers, which would indeed be a tragedy for one of the charms of the place is its clear open spaces. Much of the island is flat limestone with contours broken only by occasional heaps of stones which serve as boundary markers and by scraps of shrub stunted by the nibblings of free-roaming sheep. Oh yes, and windmills – hundreds of them – but many now abandoned and falling apart.

Öland is described as bleak by those who think the landscape is tedious, and as wild and unspoilt by those who enjoy an uncluttered horizon. But then there are also some visitors who, when asked for an opinion, reply 'what view'? Contrary to expectations these are less likely to be philistines as academic specialists who come to the island in pursuit of highly specific objectives. Leading the pack are the archaeologists, who are forever turning up new evidence of ancient habitation. There are finds from the Iron Age to the early Middle Ages with plenty of easily observable links with the Viking community including various runestones and the markings of ship burials. Above the town of Borgholm there are the ruins of a great medieval castle which defied all deliberate efforts to destroy it, surviving to the early nineteenth century when it was ravaged by fire.

Jostling the history seekers are the botanists, who appreciate Öland as the home of wild flowers seldom, if ever, found elsewhere in Scandinavia. The limestone land base and a mild dry climate create ideal conditions for colourful subtropical plants, notably blue anemones and a bewildering variety of orchids. A third group of specialists are the ornithologists, for Öland is slap on the migration route for millions of birds. Of those who pause for a rest on what they expect to be safe territory, a proportion find themselves being closely scrutinised by members of the Swedish Ornithological Society who record their vital statistics and present them with a date ring before sending them on their way.

Öland is the second largest island in Sweden; the first is its neighbour, Gotland. Eighty miles long and over thirty miles wide, Gotland is sufficiently spacious and secluded (the sea journey to the mainland is everything of four hours) to provide an ideal holiday setting for the rich and/or the famous. It is said that if you swim here in July you are as likely as not to interrupt a Cabinet meeting on the beach. The pursuit of birds and botany is almost as energetic as in Öland and there are rich archaeological discoveries. Gotland was an important base for Viking traders whose areas of business can now be estimated by correlating relics found in graves here and in Eastern Europe. It is known, for instance, that they travelled regularly to the Latvian coast. A good impression of their means of transport can be gathered from carved and painted stones on Gotland which show the evolution of sailing boats from the days when it was thought to be sufficient to tie a small piece of cloth to the mast, to the eight-century when the Vikings raised huge sails to carry the boats further, faster and more safely.

Gotland enjoys a lively tourist industry with the main interest centring on Visby – the 'town of ruins and roses'. Like Kalmar it was one of the great trading communities of the Middle Ages, when it was chiefly controlled by German merchants. But by the fourteenth century the frequency with which Gotland was made a battleground weakened Visby's appeal as a commercial haven. Its decline was precipitated by a Danish assault in 1361 which led to the massacre of a Swedish army outside the city wall. It still exists, this wall, about two miles of it between eighteen and thirty feet high with forty-four towers. Within this boundary are seventeen medieval churches, many in ruins but splendidly majestic nonetheless with their broken arches and open roofs. But to continue with the statistics would be to hammer a point that must already be obvious – that Visby is one of the most interesting medieval cities in Europe – and one of the best preserved.

There are any number of eating places on Öland and Gotland but to avoid for once the olde worlde charm favoured by the regular tourist trade let me recommend two thoroughly modern restaurants. Öland has a new steakhouse called Lammet och Grisen or The Lamb and Pig, an aptly named establishment since they roast these animals whole in the middle of the dining room. A recent addition to the south Gotland scene is Majstre Gården, a sea-view restaurant offering sea food. The speciality of the house is salmon or, more accurately, sea trout. Sightseeing at the other end of the island, you are almost certain to come across a coffee house called Bruket. Even if you forget the name of the place it is easily identifiable. For one thing they serve each customer with a basket containing coffee pot, sandwiches, cakes or whatever. Come to think of it, this is quite a sensible arrangement for a busy waitress can handle a basket a great deal easier than a tray. The other distinguishing characteristic of Bruket is that it is near the caves at Lummelunda. This subterranean network excavated by water seeping through the limestone rock is a subject of endless fascination for visitors to Gotland who enjoy nothing better than trying to remember from their school science lessons which are the stalagmites and which the stalactites.

10. Stockholm

Time now to return to the mainland to join the road to Stockholm, the tourist trail to the heart of the country and the migratory route for all Swedes in search of the high life. Our approach is through Södermanland, a province which offers a good scenic mix of forest and lakes and open hilly farm land. Across the northern boundary stretches Lake Mälaren, one of the links in the coast-to-coast wanderings of the Göta Canal. Södermanland has been called the playground of Stockholm. It has a great appeal for the weekenders in search of open-air exercise and seclusion within a reasonable travelling orbit of their urban flats. And this is not an exclusively contemporary pursuit. Affluent Stockholmers have always felt the need to escape occasionally from the environment of day-to-day business. This was as true of the society of 300 years ago as it is of our own times. The only difference is that in earlier periods affluence was a descriptive term reserved for a small minority whose idea of a modest holiday home was a spacious manor house. Stately residences are thick on the ground in Södermanland and on the islands of Lake Mälaren, though now, in the age of the levellers, many of them are owned by the state and open to the public.

A great favourite with visitors is Gripsholm, a palace built in the Renaissance but enlarged and otherwise modified by successive Swedish monarchs. One of its claims to special interest is the huge portrait collection – some 3,000 pictures in all. The last king to make a home at Gripsholm was Gustav III, whose failures in political leadership were more than compensated by his enthusiastic and generous patronage of the arts. In his twenty-year reign he founded the Swedish Academy to cultivate a national literature and established the Royal Dramatic Theatre and the Royal Opera. His love of the theatre was such that even when campaigning in the Russian War he insisted on being kept up to date on the latest productions in Stockholm. In the end he took a leading but unrehearsed role in his very own drama. At a masked ball at the Royal Opera in 1792 he was shot down by an assassin. Appropriately enough, the event inspired a Verdi opera. Gustav had a theatre built at Gripsholm and though unused since the court entertainments for Christmas 1786, it is preserved in its original state.

Another palace in a Renaissance setting much favoured by Gustav III was Drottningholm where, again, the theatre is preserved in full working order. But here the show goes on. Every summer some fifty performances from opera and ballet are staged with faithful regard to the eighteenth-century traditions. The original sets are put into service, also the antique machinery for achieving scene changes which, despite its age, functions almost as quickly and efficiently as a modern revolving stage. As a further aid to re-creating the proper atmosphere, the musicians dress in period costume and even the audience who crowd into the tiny auditorium are made to feel part of the wider act by seating themselves in places marked for members of the Royal household. The theatre is an annexe to the summer palace, which is still used as a royal residence, but with sections open to public inspection. It is conveniently close to Stockholm – less than half an hour by road, and even by boat only an hour's journey.

And so to Stockholm itself – the Venice of the North (for all but the Dutch, who built Amsterdam likewise) – over some twenty islands which are spread out like stepping stones between Lake Mälaren and the sea. First impressions of the city depend on the season. Stockholm is beautiful – everyone agrees to that – but in the last months of the year when the temperature hovers on freezing point and the two ends of day rush to meet one another at around noon, an awful gloom descends. The city is in mourning for the loss of summer and the streets are filled with miserable-looking Swedes telling each other how miserable it is to be miserable. With the new year the public mood changes radically. Everyone cheers up in anticipation of Spring when Stockholm is far and away at her best. The air is cool, clean and dry – ideal for exploring the urban scene but particularly so for Stockholm which seems to have been purpose built for the pedestrian. Stockholm is the wanderer's delight. It is a small, compact, neatly patterned city, in which it is almost impossible for the stranger to lose himself for more than a few minutes. So, leave the car in the hotel garage (you won't find another decent parking space anyway), throw away the tourist brochures, refuse all offers of coach tours and just start walking.

Say you begin at the Central Station, a fair assumption since most of the larger hotels are in the vicinity. Half left or straight ahead from this formidable grey slab of a building are the major shopping streets – notably Kungsgatan, Drottinggatan and Klarabersgatan – with their eminently inviting department stores such as Åhléns and PUB. Stockholm retailers share a great ability for creating eye-catching displays even for quite mundane products. If my own experience is typical, their effort is commercially beneficial since always I come away with purchases for which hitherto I have never felt any compelling need. The most recent extravagance inspired by a need to get my shoes repaired made me the owner of a pair of clogs, a style of footwear popular in Sweden but which somehow seems out of place in my part of London. Funny I did not think of that at the time. Craft products – wood, textile and pottery – are everywhere and there is a wide choice of good-quality glass and jewellery, the latter often moderately priced, presumably because so much of it is produced by young artists trying to break into the market.

If, while window-gazing in the area, you happen to take a few short cuts down the narrow side streets you will almost certainly discover the notorious sex shop district, which is worth a visit if only to discover what most Swedes have known for generations – that sex in the raw is terribly boring unless you happen to be one of the participants.

The top of Klarabergsgatan is the approach to new Stockholm, identified by an intersection of broad thoroughfares and in this sea of tarmac, an island of water, spiked in the middle by an obelisk sculptured in glass. Just below road level is a square which is popular with demonstrators and other performers and this is faced by the House of Culture, a blessed refuge for weary explorers who want time off to read a book or the newspapers or listen to a record or simply to sit and stare over a cup of coffee. Part of the complex is the temporary base for the Swedish Parliament – though why the members would ever think of moving again is difficult to understand since they are provided with every possible luxury including private flats and, would you believe, a meditation room? The area is known as Sergels Torg, which is a bow in the direction of the eighteenth-century sculptor Johan Tobias Sergel, who lived and worked nearby. The terrible irony is that his studio was demolished to make way for this new development, an act of ruthlessness which was quite typical of the heavy mob who dominated planning in the sixties. Close by are the Höghusen or the high houses, the set of five tower blocks which have served as a model for other commercial buildings soon to arise from the craters that spatter the landscape in this part of the city. But some of the old associations have survived. There is still a market at Hötorget, though nowadays the dealers in hay who gave the square its name are no longer to be found among the stall holders. On one side of the square is the Concert Hall, a 1920s building which was originally light blue then declined to dull grey and is now restored to its original cheerful colour. Decorating, or rather dominating the entrance – surprise, surprise – is a Milles fountain. The Hall is fronted by ten Corinthian columns and a great flight of steps which, in summer, serve as meeting and talking place for half the young people in Stockholm.

Straight ahead from Sergels Torg is NK, the Harrods of Stockholm, where virtually anything can be bought – at a price. The Swedes enjoy nothing better than an occasional burst of extravagance, and NK is just the place for them to work off their exuberance. The cash registers ring up the sales at typewriter speed, as the classless society discover things they never knew they wanted until NK showed them the possibilities. If such a comment were made about some stores in any other European capital, the cry of consumer exploitation would he heard in the streets. And rightly so, for so much effort goes into persuading the shopper that good money should be spent on rubbish. But in Sweden the argument has much less force. Value for money is a phrase that has kept its meaning, quality is not a sad and abused word, and new ideas really are new ideas, not simply attempts to revive interest in standard products by giving them a shiny plastic veneer.

Opposite NK is the Swedish House where invariably there is a design exhibition worth visiting. On the ground floor the tourist information service deals out general information while upstairs there is library of books on Sweden and a small shop specialising in multilingual publications, mostly from the Swedish Institute, on social and economic topics. The restaurant here is popular with visitors but standards are variable and it is wise to check if Stockholmers are patronising the place before booking a table. The Swedish House overlooks Kungsträdgården, which is called a park but is more like a good old-fashioned promenade with cafés, a bandstand, statues among the flower beds and fountains and, most intriguing, giant chess games which require the players to walk across the broad to make their moves. There are some complaints that the hippies are too much in evidence but one of the wonders of the Stockholm scene is that while the youngsters can be as wildly exuberant as anywhere, there are few signs of vandalism or other anti-social behaviour. Among the attractions of Kungsträdgarden are the displays of design and craftwork set out in glass showcases. It may be that a few breakages occur but if this is so the repair services are brought in very fast indeed. More probably the general respect for public property extends to these fragile items as much as to sturdier constructions which are refreshingly clean and unspoilt by the graffiti artists.

For the second stage of the tour we start again at the Central Station, turning right at the main exit to walk towards a traffic flyover and the Sheraton Hotel – the largest in Stockholm. Negotiate a few road crossings (and please, please wait until the flashing signs give the all clear, because of all places in Sweden the police in Stockholm are the quickest in nabbing and fining pedestrians who jump the lights) and then ahead you will see – well, actually, you will see water, which is the commonest feature of the city scene. Before talking more about buildings it might be as well to cast a respectful glance in the direction of Strömmen – literally, Current – the fast-moving funnel of water which connects Lake Mälaren with the Baltic. In winter when a cold crisp wind flips the surface, Strömmen can be an unfriendly companion but in the warm months there is the cosy relaxation of watching the patterns of the stream as it chases along the shore and spits off the bows of oncoming boats. Incredibly for a central city waterway Strömmen attracts fishermen and, though the catch is not greatly exciting, there are some characters who continue to make a full-time job of scooping out a few marine commuters. They work with a round net which hangs from a spar on the end of the boat. The ploy is to drop the net, drift a few yards, then pull in and hope for the best.

Holding a position on the left bank of Strömmen, the choice of direction for the sightseer is wide open. On one side, the City Hall, symbol of the emergence of Swedish self-confidence early in the century when it was still the thing to judge civic pride by the size and richness of a banqueting chamber. A flat, red-brick building, it is far less pretentious outside than in, a characteristic which allows the experts to designate it as a breakthrough to modern Swedish design. To the left is the Opera House, a total contrast in style and a reminder of the

Ape of Liberty when Gustav III was projecting artistic licence to its full stretch.

On the far bank of Strömmen are the stately facades of the Old Parliamentary House and some of the government buildings erected in a frenzy of eighteenth-century architectural extravagance; the Royal Palace and the boundary houses of the Old Town known locally as Gamla Stan. This is the real centre of Stockholm for it was here 700 years ago that the city was born. A fortress with outbuildings was erected 'very stoutly and pleasantly' according to *Erik's Chronicle* by Berger Paul, a nobleman whose origins are obscure, but whose power was evidently considerable. He chose his defensive position wisely since the site of the Old Town is a small, high-rise island which must have offered a commanding view over all approaches. No trace of the fortress survives but some of the houses built at about the same time can still be seen. They stand between Österlånggatan and Västerlånggatan (the latter is now the district's main shopping street and called the Longest Store in Stockholm) which mark the line of the wall that encircled medieval Stockholm. Most of the other houses in the Old Town span the period from the sixteenth to the eighteenth centuries but, even where relatively modern buildings predominate, the medieval pattern of construction is still apparent with thin, tightly framed houses facing on to the narrow cobbled streets and alleys (the narrowest, Mårten Trotzigs Gränd, is only a yard wide) that lead down to the water's edge. A few years ago the Old Town was sadly dilapidated and thought by some to be in need of the sort of ruthless planning and redevelopment treatment that has destroyed the character of many of Sweden's historic centres. Fortunately this came at just about the time when it dawned on civic leaders that much of what is old, if treated with care and respect, can actually enhance the virtues of modern living. Thus millions of kronor were spent on giving the Old Town a facelift with the result that it became a highly desirable residential area, particularly for artists and craftsmen. It is now a model exercise in conservation, an historical showcase and a centre of frantic cultural and commercial activity. Mercifully, it is also virtually traffic-free. The Old Town contains some of the best restaurants in Stockholm – names like Fem Små Hus, Gyllene Freden, Aurora, Diana and Catellin are instantly recognisable by anyone in the city who enjoys a meal out. But, at the risk of repetition, bear in mind that the Swedes eat early in the evening and that standards are liable to decline dramatically the closer you book to midnight.

A popular gathering point in the Old Town is Stortorget or the Great Square which is flanked on one side by the Stock Exchange, now also a meeting place for the Swedish Academy and the home of the Nobel Library. There are usually a few market stalls but business is quiet and the almost cloister atmosphere appealing to those who like to take things gently makes it difficult to believe that Stortorget has a place in Swedish history as the scene of an infamous demonstration in cold-blooded violence. It was here in 1520 that the Danish king, Christian II removed final opposition to his claim to Swedish territory by the simple but ruthless expedient of chopping off the heads of some eighty nobles and two bishops.

Another reminder of the mailed fist which dominated early Swedish power politics is Riddarholm Church on the tiny island of Riddarholmen (Island of the Knights) at the edge of the Old Town. This green-domed structure with its commanding iron latticed tower accommodates the remains of Sweden's battling monarchs, notably Gustavus Adolphus, the revolutionary in military tactics who transformed the Swedish army into a highly profitable export by offering, for ample consideration, to fight anyone, anywhere; and Charles XII, imperialist extraordinary whose corpse has twice been exhumed in the so far fruitless effort to determine if he died honourably or was shot by rivals in his own camp when he attacked the Norwegian fortress of Fredrikshald in 1718. Also in Riddarholmen is the Wrangel Palace which served as the official royal residence in the early eighteenth century. In front is a statue of Birger Jarl. Close by is Riddarhuset, or House of

Nobles, built in the mid-seventeenth century by Gustavus Adolphus, who decided that if the aristocracy were so keen to participate in government they might as well have somewhere to meet and deliberate. The main hall in the building displays over 2,000 coats of arms including that of Sven Hedin, the explorer and last man in Sweden to be knighted.

Still on the boundary of the Old Town, but more on the north side, the Royal Palace dominates the scene. There is certainly nothing fancy about this massive grey granite-faced residence but its sharp outline and sheer size give it an unmistakeable regal dignity. Seen from across the water it is a marvellous spectacle. The Palace is unlike royal homes elsewhere in Europe in that it is immediately accessible. The King can walk out of his front door on to one of the busiest streets in Stockholm and, by the same token, the public can walk in if they have a mind to inspect some of the 550 rooms that are maintained at their expense. The decoration and furnishings, which are more extravagant and much richer than might be expected in a Swedish setting, are the product of French cultural influence in the early eighteenth century.

The Palace itself dates from the same period, it being the successor to the medieval Castle of Three Crowns which was destroyed by fire in 1697 when it was in the process of being reconstructed. The rubble from the old building was heaped up on the north side to form a steap hill known as Lejonbacken, or the Lion's Hill, after the pair of bronze lions at the foot of the slope. The metal for the handsome beasts was stolen from Denmark in the shape of a fountain which used to stand in front of Kronberg Castle at Elsinore.

Fortunately, Stockholm's cathedral (Storkyrkan or St Nicholas' Church) which is just across the way, escaped the flames which obliterated the Castle of Three Crowns. This is the oldest survivor of the district, mostly fifteenth-century but with parts dating back another 200 years. Casual strollers tend to bypass Storkyrkan since its dull brown-plaster exterior does not promise much in the way of internal embellishment but the fact that many of the big ceremonies of state such as royal weddings take place here, hints at something exceptional.

There is a magnificent central altar made of black ebony (called, curiously enough, The Silver Altar) which immediately catches attention but nestling behind red brick Gothic columns there are a succession of treasures. The huge medieval wooden sculpture of St George slaying the Dragon commemorates the Battle of Brunkeberg in 1471 – one of the major events in Swedish history – when Stockholm was saved from a Danish invasion and national independence was established as the dominant political movement. Near the front entrance hangs the earliest painting of Stockholm, which shows the tiny walled city of the 1530s surrounded then by uninhabited and heavily wooded islands.

But the authentic atmosphere of the Old Town has little to do with public monuments, however impressive. What gives the place its special character are the leaning houses, and little streets and the quayside – Skeppsbron – which is lined up with modern cruising ships but still has that well-worn look about it suggesting that if a four-masted schooner put into port it would not look out of place. Not long ago when all the boats to Finland left from here, the quay was often crowded with happy Stockholmers preparing to embark on two- or three-day cruises. The popularity of these trips, most of which now start from waterfronts that are less traffic-congested, increases every year. There are some proud and upright Swedes who will tell you that this shipping success story proves the bonds of friendship between Nordic states. But the sordid truth is that the overwhelming majority of Stockholmers who take to the boats do so because they know that once out of harbour the tax regulations on drink and other designated 'luxury' items are miraculously lifted. Then it's a case of eat, drink and buy everything below standard price for tomorrow the long arm of the taxman will once more be stretching out to grab us. The Swedes who have worked out the economies of the short-term cruise to a fine art do not even bother to go the full journey but stop off at Åland, an

13 *Stockholm's City Hall.*

inhabited slab of red Finish rock about equidistant from both countries. Everything that needs to be bought and is unobtainable on the boat – such as meat – can be purchased on Åland. But if you intend joining one of these convivial shopping sprees be prepared for some rough patches at sea. It is not unknown for a newcomer to discover that the combined effects of a good smörgåsbord, cheap schnapps and a heaving boat can put paid to the firmest resolutions to search out bargains on the mainland.

Working on the assumption that exploring the Old Town stimulates a need to find out more about Stockholm's history, the next stop is Skeppsholmen, the neighbouring island downstream from Gamla stan. It was once a naval base but the only signs now of the military presence are a set of well-oiled cannons pointing ominously at Skeppsbron but which, I am assured, are used only to salute important visitors arriving by sea. Indeed there is not even very much in the way of shipping except a nineteenth-century windjammer which is now at permanent anchor and serves as a youth hostel. It is called *af Chapman*, after the great eighteenth-century shipbuilder of English descent whose yards were spread over the island. Skeppsholmen has turned from the art of defence to the defence of art, the most sturdy-looking building being reserved for exhibiting the work of the modern school of painters. A permanent open-air display of sculptures which incorporates pieces of machinery – in working order – is very popular with the children and may even prove something about art such as, with enough cheek you can get away with murder. Just over the bridge connecting Skeppsholmen to the Blasieholmen peninsula is the National Gallery, a sober and heavy building designed more with an eye to the width of the central staircase and the height of the ceilings than to the practicalities of hanging pictures. But the collection is impressive and surprisingly representative, which is not to be patronising but merely to acknowledge that until the last century Sweden was far removed from the great centres of European culture. A few steps on is another building which it

14 One of the narrow streets in Stockholm's Old Town.

is impossible not to notice. The 100-year-old Grand Hotel, directly overlooking Strömmen and facing the Royal Palace has, by external appearances, all the pretensions of one of those nineteenth-century international clubs for tired aristocrats on the European tour. But the Grand has adapted to the times and now, thoroughly modernised, puts stronger emphasis on comfort than on class. One of the happy surprises for a visitor to Stockholm is to discover that the Grand offers one of the best and least expensive smörgåsbord in the entire city. Near the Grand are the pleasure boats which, throughout the summer, do the round tours of the Stockholm waterways and take the Stockholmers to their weekend cottages in the archipelago.

From Skeppsholmen and its environs to a much larger island – Djurgården described by Bellman as an 'isle of pleasure' though whether he was thinking of the natural beauty of the place or his social experiences is not at all clear. At one time it was a royal deer-hunting park, which accounts for the heavy population of trees, but now, though Djurgården still has the reputation of being something quite apart from the commercial and residential development of the city, it is no longer remote or inaccessible. Millions of people visit the island each year and most of them come because they want to see Skansen, one of the most remarkable historical exhibitions in Europe.

Opened in 1891, Skansen is quite simply the first open-air museum but, if for you museum conjures up images of serried ranks of exhibits all neatly catalogued and labelled but otherwise unrelated and somehow isolated from their own and the present time, then prepare for a revelation. Skansen is more, much more than that. It is an attempt to present a bird's eye view of the development of Sweden by re-creating social and economic conditions from various periods of history, and from different parts of the country. Thus, a visitor can find himself wandering into an eighteenth-century town centre, a farm from Skåne, a manor house, a Norrland homestead, or a Lappish nomadic settlement all carefully and accurately pieced together from original items saved in one place or another from the rush into modernisation, and the attention of the demolition squads. And these buildings are not empty shells. There are craftsmen at work and the shops are open for business. In the rural section, the farms are populated by real animals and the butter and cheese are made in just the way that great grandmother recommended. If the tourists wore traditional costume, the historical cameo would be complete.

Skansen was the brain child of Arthur Harelius, the founder of the nearby Nordiska Museet (Nordic Museum), which also claims to depict the life and work of the Swedish people but is more formally academic in its style of presentation. The two organisations are linked administratively, and in many ways their work is complementary – a large section of the Museum staff are out researching Sweden's home craft tradition and folk culture. But from early days (the Nordiska Museet was established nearly twenty years earlier than its partner) Skansen has had a special claim to popular support by representing the history of all of the people for all of the people. Dedicated to the idea that history can be fun Skansen has gradually broadened its terms of reference to become an entertainment centre offering concerts, folk dancing and music, restaurants, a huge play area for children (Lill-Skansen) and a zoo.

Skansen is the model for numerous ventures elsewhere in Europe and in America but nowhere has the idea been taken up with such enthusiasm as in Sweden. Nowadays, almost every important urban centre has its own version of Skansen – often no more than a few restored wooden houses accommodating small exhibitions and craft demonstrations, but sometimes an ambitious project in conservation enhancing, as, for instance, at Linköping, an entire section of what is left of the old town which now serves as living accommodation, work area and retail outlet for the arts and crafts fraternity. But popular acceptance of the Skansen principle has brought its own problems. Critics point out that urban planners whose passion for things modern is apparently boundless, can make use of the local open-air museums as dumping grounds for historic buildings which they might otherwise be pressurised into maintaining in their original setting. Hopefully, this danger is subsiding as environmental questions take stronger hold on the public and administrative imagination.

Another great attraction of Djurgården is the Wasa, the seventeenth-century warship which turned turtle at the beginning of its maiden voyage and rested at the bottom of the harbour for three centuries. The wreck was located in 1956 and lifted five years later. The remarkable story of how this vessel and many of its original contents were brought to the surface is in the best tradition of real-life adventures. Some idea of just how much engineering skill and scientific expertise went into the operation can be judged immediately on entering the museum especially erected for the Wasa, since even now the ship must be constantly sprayed with a solution of polyethylene glycol to prevent the timbers from rotting. It is a weird sight, a reminder of tales of ghost ships emerging from the mist, only this is real and the mist is the protective spray advancing in waves across the decks.

Djurgården has an amusement park called Gröna Lund a canal which in summer is crowded with small boats, a number of small specialist museums and even an art gallery. A recommended keep-fit exercise is to try to cover the lot in a single day.

The way to the southern sector of Stockholm is via Slussen, which means lock or sluice. Taken literally the name describes what was, rather than what is there now, for while many years ago a complicated series of locks controlled the major exit to the archipelago, today a single lock crouches under a gigantic cloverleaf spread of elevated roads from which the traffic can spin off in seven directions. Anticipating a sniff of indifference to what, after all, is a fairly common feature of most big cities, Stockholmers quickly point out that Slussen was opened in the 1930s, some while before urbanites elsewhere even recognised that traffic congestion was a cumulative problem.

The south or Södermalm is instantly recognisable by its high boundary ridge of sheer rock rising over Slussen. One way of avoiding a steep drive or walk to the top is to take the Katarina lift which has been saving the energy of Stockholmers since 1886. A good head for heights is needed, for you will be travelling in an open shaft. It used to be said that the Katarina offered the best view over the city but this proud distinction now belongs to Kaknästornet, the 300-foot communications tower just north of the Djurgården area. Until a few years ago Södermalm was virtually an independent sector, its citizenry proudly working-class, speaking their own impenetrable Swedish slang. But vast rebuilding programmes have obliterated much of the old character of the district and it needs patient effort to search out the few remaining wooden and yellow-brick cottages. Restored and modernised, these have acquired great charm and are immensely popular with artists and craftsmen – the non-conformists in Swedish society.

By European standards Stockholm is an open and spacious city but Stockholmers are not comforted by this knowledge. They give the impression that they are gasping for air as the growing multitude of buildings and vehicles close in on them. This is a serious psychological illness which has only one possible cure – frequent and regular opportunities to get the hell out of it. A trip to the weekend cottage is, as we know, a much favoured remedy for urban weariness but another antidote with perhaps even greater appeal is boating. Anyone who stays long in Stockholm will inevitably be invited to join a sailing expedition. What this usually means in practice is a day trip to the archipelago with a picnic and sun bathing on one of the islands. There is absolutely no danger of overcrowding here, since there are well over 20,000 islands in the vicinity ranging from small outcrops of smooth, bald rock serving as rest areas for itinerant seagulls to thickly wooded stretches of land, which, if they were more heavily populated, look large enough to claim independence. If you are not skilled at navigating small craft and nervous at sitting a few inches above the waves, have some faith in the competence of the waterbound Swede who treats his boat with respect and an understanding of its limitations. Then again, nature has thoughtfully provided an additional safety measure by declaring this a non-tidal area and, even when currents are strong or rough weather blows up, there is always the consolation of knowing that land is not far away. Of the two million or so who regularly go out sailing only about 150 a year suffer fatal accidents, and it is said that a high proportion of these forgot the golden rule – never drink and sail.

Organised commercial cruises lasting anything from an hour or to a whole day can be equally pleasurable. Tourism has kept alive the coastal passenger business and a busy shuttle service of steamers tour the island routes. For the longer trips the ships are equipped for the full service including a decent, if simple meal, called Steamer Beefsteak which was the favourite dish in the days when water transport was an essential line of communication. Even the quick outings round central Stockholm are a worthwhile experience for so much of the city is built from an architect's image of what looks best and most impressive from the water. Hearing the guide's commentary four times in different languages can be a little wearisome but the burden is minimised by a strict regard for brevity and a welcome lightness of style. 'That's the British Embassy.' I once heard a guide inform his audience. 'We usually manage to arrange for the Rolls Royce to be in the drive but at least you can see the roses round the door.'

11. Vacationland

Stockholm has been the first city in Sweden for so long it is difficult to believe that other communities should once have claimed the role of leader. Yet, not far from the capital, are two retired competitors either of which, but for an accident of history, might have grasped the power of national government. On Lake Mälaren is the island of Björkö, quiet and secluded now but once a great trading centre patronised by Europeans and Orientals. Little remains of Birka, the island town, but in Viking times it was a magnet for the rest of the country and might properly be described as Sweden's first capital. It went into decline before A.D. 1000, probably the victim of Danish raiders who compelled the business people to look elsewhere for a peaceful market place. They left behind them remnants of their civilization, including some 2,000 grave mounds which have subsequently provided a fruitful source of information for the archaeologists.

Much of the Birka's trade was transferred to Sigtuna on the eastern shore of Lake Mälaren. Here, too, a period of rapid growth was terminated by invaders. No longer exercising any commercial or political influence Sigtuna has at least managed to survive in recognisable shape, a jumble of medieval streets and ruined churches. As one of the earliest Christian communities in the country the town has retained strong links with the Church. The Lutherans have their own schools and adult study centres in Sigtuna and religious conferences are a regular feature in the local calendar. Birka and Sigtuna had lost their claim to pre-eminence long before the founding fathers of Stockholm were really into their stride.

But a few miles to the north was a potential rival with an already proved capacity for thriving in a changeable political climate. Uppsala, originally called Östra Aros, was the capital of the ancient kingdom of the Svear whose power, predating that of the Vikings, is thought to have extended over most of the then inhabited parts of Sweden. Just outside the modern city of Uppsala are three great mounds marking the graves of Svear kings. In the days when those gentlemen were active, the area accommodated a temple dedicated to the three heathen gods, Tor, Odin and Frey. Tor ruled the air and the elements, Odin was the God of War, and Frey, who inspired the most heart-felt and enthusiastic devotion, was the God of Fertility. It was customary to make a live sacrifice to Frey at the time of a wedding and, if this implies an awful lot of blood letting, bear in mind that routine festivals in the pagan almanac required the slaughter of nine males to every creature in the vicinity – dogs, horses, cattle and humans. To complete this gruesome picture the law stated that the remains of the victims should be hung in a sacred grave.

Sweden was the last of the Scandinavian countries to abandon the pagan traditions, and even in the eleventh century the traveller Adam of Bremen was able to compile a lengthy catalogue of heathen customs still practised in the country. But ironically, when Christianity began to take hold of the popular imagination it was Uppsala provided the main launching base for the new religion. The first cathedral, completed by King Erik, who was to become patron saint of Sweden, was built on the site of the pagan temple. It was Erik who, on receiving news that the Danes were attacking, insisted on concluding his prayers before going to battle. This act of piousness secured his canonisation but failed to ensure his earthly survival. He was cut down by an enemy axe in 1160. The name Uppsala first appears in the records in the late thirteenth century when the city became the seat of the Primate of Sweden. At this time work started on the present cathedral, where what is left of Erik is preserved in a silver casket. Also accommodated are the remains of Gustav Vasa, the 'founder of modern Sweden', among whose achievements must be counted the building of the castle at Uppsala. A sombre and imposing setting for historical events, the castle witnessed in 1654 the abdication of Queen Christina, daughter of Gustavus Adolphus. She, it was, who earned a reputation as a pioneer of sex equality by insisting on taking her royal oath as king, a demand conceded by the establishment without too much bother. But she overstepped the limits of public indulgence when she turned Catholic. Christina must go insisted the Lutheran nobility – and she went, saying that was what she wanted to do anyway. She spent the rest of her life in Rome in a house once occupied by St. Bridget of Vadstena.

Today, the castle is the residence of the governor of Uppland, the province of which Uppsala is the capital. One of the previous occupants of this post was the father of Dag Hammarskjöld who spent his childhood here. The castle has changed character and shape since it inauguration. It was finished in the mid-seventeenth century but was badly damaged by fire in 1702 and had to be largely reconstructed. Similarly the cathedral, though unmistakable Gothic, has been subjected to many alterations and renovations over the years, the last in the 1890s when the twin towers were raised to a height of nearly 400 feet.

These two contrasting monuments – the castle moulded to the brow of a hill like a giant limpet, and the cathedral, slender and pinnacled, dominate the skyline of Uppsala. The character of the city, however, owes more to the university, another institution with an impressive history but livelier now that it has ever been. The foundation, dating from 1477, has branched into every part of the city, and the original accommodation where it still exists has changed its function radically over the years. One of the oldest buildings, the Gustavanum, now used for art exhibitions was once better-known as a place where medical students tried their hand at anatomical dissection, and the old jailhouse near the cathedral still caters for students, but as a restaurant. The library, containing over a million volumes and 20,000 manuscripts, is the largest in Sweden.

Like other ancient universities in Europe, Uppsala is beset by traditions, the chief of which require the students to indulge in eccentric behaviour for the general and, presumably, their own entertainment. The performance of the year takes place on 30 April, the eve of the first day of spring, better known in Sweden as Walpurgis Eve. This is when the students must wear their white caps – symbol of intellectual status – and gather before the library. At three in the afternoon the signal is given for the commencement of an organised riot which consists of the mass of students rushing wildly down the main street to the river. It is said that a few over-enthusiastic participants attempt the return journey up the hill while the majority of their colleagues are still completing the first stage. There is no confirmation of anyone covering the entire route but this may be because by the time the victors come out of hospital the onlookers and judges have lost interest. The rest of Walpurgis Eve, for those who are still in fit condition, consists of singing, dancing, eating and drinking – often simultaneously.

Uppsala has experienced considerable industrialisation and housing development over recent years – an inevitable progression, perhaps, but one that has destroyed, unnecessarily, some of the more attractive features of the city. Everyone has their own pet examples of authorised vandalism but they add up to a loss of hundreds of old buildings many of which had strong historical associations.

If Uppland is the nucleus of Swedish civilization – and the evidence of the rune stones which abound in this part of the country is alone strong enough to show that it all started here – then Dalarna, one of the neighbouring provinces, is the heart of the nation. Anyway, that is what the local inhabitants claim, though they hasten to point out that, geographically speaking, the dead centre is somewhat to the north of their territory. What they have in mind is that Dalarna, the fourth largest province, offers an almost totally representative spread of Swedish landscape from mixed farming to mountains and thick pine forest. From the south comes the cry 'us to', for here Dalarna joins with Värmland, another large province characterised by forest and lakes and red farmhouses, all of which figure prominently in the romantically idyllic writing of Selma Lageröf, the first woman to be awarded the Nobel Prize for Literature. Värmland and Dalarna both have the credit for keeping alive the old peasant traditions. They are encouraged by a mighty incursion of holiday makers who enjoy nothing more than a gentle reminder of the Sweden of their grandparents. The art and craft industry flourishes as never before and the Dalarna horse, a wooden sculpture sold in souvenir shops throughout the country, is probably more immediately recognisable internationally than the Swedish flag.

Carving horses has been a local business for well over a century. Originally, there was as many shapes, sizes and colours of the beast as there were families who wanted to earn a little extra money or occupy their time in the long autumn and winter evenings. Now, the manufacturing process is much simplified with production concentrated at Nusnäs, a small village east of Mora, and there are standard colours for the model — white with blue spots or brick red. But mass production has been kept at bay which is only to be expected in a region where the old-fashioned ways make sound commercial sense. The people of the villages even retain their own folk-costumes which, neatly dry cleaned, are brought out and donned for every festival. Come midsummer, that great celebration, the fiddlers play country music as long as the dancers are prepared to swing round the may poles. Nothing changes, except that now the tourists gather in crowds to watch the spectacle.

Dalarna's best-favoured tourist region is the Lake Siljan valley with its three little rustic towns — Rättvik. Leksand and Mora. The last of these was the home of Anders Zorn, an impressionist painter of world-wide reputation whose life spanned the turn of the century. Zorn was a great collector — of his own and other people's art, of peasant craft work and locally designed furniture and even of farm buildings, an assembly of which is still preserved and on show at Mora. The Zorn museum and home contains most of his acquisitions and there is a comprehensive display of his famous paintings – many of them featuring those nude and gorgeously plump country girls who are immensely popular with postcard buyers but who, it must be sadly admitted, would not win any prizes at a Swedish dieticians' conference.

Another much loved Dalarna painter is Carl Larsson whose idealistic interpretation of rural life in the last century was discussed earlier in the context of folk traditions. But the point must be made here that the contemporary preoccupation with peasant culture is as much as anything an extension of the images created by Larsson. All the time the emphasis is on simple and natural happiness, an artistic purpose which may not lend itself to sophisticated analysis but, as most Swedes would readily agree, is none the worse for that.

But I must not give the impression that either Dalarna or Värmland are entirely averse to making a livelihood from modern technology. Among the big firms based here is Bofors, the armaments and engineering company brought to international prominence by Alfred Nobel. Wood and pulp are highly organised and highly productive industries and straddling the southern boundaries of both regions is the rich iron-ore district of Bergslagen, where the output curve is rising despite a great number of pit closures. In Falun there is Stora Kopparbergs Bergslags AB, one of the oldest trading companies in the world. Its prosperity was founded on a copper mine which has been turning out quantities of rich ore ever since the twelfth century.

There is not much pure copper left now, indeed the mine started on its decline 200 years ago, but subsidiary products such as the red ochre which is used to protect the wood of so many farm houses, keeps the business alive. The tourists come here to see a vast open pit caused by earth collapse in the days when miners risked their lives every time they started chipping away at the rock face, and they hear a macabre but compelling story about a young man who died under a roof fall in 1677 and was found forty years later almost perfectly preserved. He was brought to the surface and identified by an old woman who recognised the still young features of a lover she once planned to marry.

To enter Dalarna and its neighbouring provinces to the north – Härjedalen and Jämtland – is to discover skiing country. Skiing is immensely popular in Sweden and all young people are taught that sliding about on two planks is not only a source of pleasure but a great opportunity for breathing fresh air and indulging in healthy exercise – the twin life savers which are thought to be the major contributory factor to the rapidly growing proportion of hearty old-age pensioners. But do not go away with the idea that all Swedes are capable of weaving out a course down the steepest slopes. Indeed the prevailing fashion is to avoid the fancy tricks in favour of tackling cross-country routes which can appeal as much to the mood of the relaxed wanderer as to the needs of the energy-consuming keep-fit enthusiast. One of the leading events in the skiing calendar is a cross-country pursuit known as the Vasa Race which starts at Sälen close to the Norwegian border and ends up fifty-five miles later at Mora in Dalarna. The event which takes place on the first Sunday in March commemorates the occasion 450 years ago when Gustav Vasa, on the run from his Danish enemies, appealed to the people of Mora to help him lead a counter attack. At first they refused and Gustav Vasa departed in search of a friendlier reception but then refugees from Stockholm turned up and the Dalarna peasants changed their mind. They went off in pursuit of the man they now wanted as leader and caught up with him at Sälen. Every year more skiers enter the race and the number of competitors now runs into thousands. To win is to achieve national fame; to finish the course is to gain admiration from family and friends and an ever interesting topic of conversation.

The top skiing resort in Härjedalen is Hamrafjället where there is an excellent hotel catering for fishermen and hunters as well as for those who come for the snow and the smooth, broad skiing slopes. Until recently Härjedalen was virtually unknown to tourists and, with a small and widely scattered population, it was dubbed 'the province that God hid away'. Times are changing rapidly but even now there is no community in the region which could possibly be described as anything more than a large village. Jämtland has had longer experience as a vacation area. The major town is Östersund and though hastening to explain a relative term by adding that the population is less than 30,000, most of the important services are here, including an airport. The athletically inclined holiday makers set their sights on Vålådalen, a favoured training area for runners who need to test their capacity for high-altitude performance. There are provisions for just about every outdoor sport from mountaineering and hiking to fishing and swimming. Another popular tourist resort is Storlien though here it is skiing that has the predominant appeal. Situated between two mountains there are slopes to suit the seasoned performer and the beginner, two groups fairly balanced in numbers who, surprisingly, have no difficulty in mixing together. Perhaps it is that in Sweden no-one feels self-conscious the first time they strap on the skis because they believe that skiing is as natural as walking. Anyone can do it and if you happen to break a leg – well, you could just as easily do that crossing the road.

Up country from Jämtland is the officially designated north of Sweden variously defined nowadays as vacation land, or Europe's last wilderness, or, more frequently by people who live there all the year round, the unemployment sector. The industrial belt is mainly to the east and we will come to that a little later but it must be said immediately that in recent years Sweden has experienced a huge migration as workers have moved closer to the thriving and wealthy Stockholm orbit. Thus, the three northernmost provinces – Lappland, Norrbotten and Västerbotten – account for one third of Sweden's total land area but only one-twentieth of its population. The leading industry is timber and pulp and though a great source of national wealth, by no stretch of imagination could it be described as labour-intensive. Holiday and sporting facilities are plentiful, and well-organised of course, but they barely intrude on an apparently limitless view of wooded mountains, river valleys and lakes. Paradoxically, as the number of people living in the far north declines, so the Swedes intensify their affection for the great outdoors. They don't want to live in isolation but they do find it immensely comforting to know that when the need arises they can get away from it all. For urban man the north epitomises the great romantic ideal. And it *is* romantic – at least for those with plenty of time and money to spare. Just think of the possibilities. A winter holiday in the middle of summer! Skiing in the light of the midnight sun – dressed in a bathing costume, of course! A brisk work-out on the slopes followed by a swim in the lake! Admittedly, these are experiences restricted to those who reach for the very top of the country. At Riksgränsen, which nudges the border with Norway, the Hotel Lapplandia employs a squad of instructors who spend all their working hours teaching guests how to ski and to acquire a suntan simultaneously. The touch of exclusiveness comes with the offer of a helicopter ride over the mountains for those who are not prepared for the exertion of a cross country trek.

Another popular tourist collecting point is Abisko, some way down from Riksgränen, near Kiruna, but still 200 kilometres inside the Arctic Circle. The summer weather is that same extraordinary mix of sun and snow but here there is the added appeal of rich and colourful vegetation which thrives on the wind-free mountain slopes. There are visitors to Abisko who come for no other reason than to search for rare plants. Then there are the hikers who use Abisko as a starting point for a leisurely cross-country trek. The routes are clearly marked and there is little danger of getting lost even on the longest stretches. The main problem would seem to be holding out for the full distance – or knowing where to stop. One set of check points known as the Royal Trail lead all the way down to Dalarna via the mountains of west Lapland 800 kilometres of steady walking. Another famous trail is the Lake Route which spans the system of lakes along the Great Lule River in north-western Lapland.

Of course, it is not essential to follow the signposts. Indeed, there are occasions when they are positively forbidden – when, for instance, walkers are engaging in that uniquely Swedish sport, orienteering. The idea is to use compass and map to find your way from one control point to another over an otherwise unmarked course. The competitor with the fastest time is the winner but participants are not always eager to achieve breakneck speeds. It can be just as entertaining an experience to work out the problems at an easy-going pace especially if children or older folk are in the party. Orienteering is gaining popularity in Europe and in the United States but the chances of planning the more complicated and exciting routes are so much better in Sweden than almost anywhere else.

Skiers, hikers, fishermen and hunters have no problem in finding accommodation to suit their needs, but if the comfort of a good-class hotel room or chalet are required advance booking is advisable. A point here is that the high life as associated with, say, the big resorts of Switzerland is not so common in Sweden. In most places the keep-fit exercises come first,with socialising a firm second, so do not, as a matter of course, expect fabulous parties every evening. The Swedes only behave like that when they are abroad. Sooner or later you will be invited to try a sauna. This is likely to happen anywhere in Sweden but in the holiday residences of the north the sauna is virtually compulsory. If it is a new experience, the first rule to keep in mind, is, don't worry. There is no medical evidence to suggest that the sauna has adversely affected the Scandinavian death rate though I am the first to admit that the mere thought of roasting the body prior to a cold shower or a roll in the snow can easily lead one to believe the contrary. Curiously it does not take long to switch from apprehension to enthusiasm. Whether or not you will actually be healthier

15 *The mountain pass known as the Lapp Gate.*

after a sauna is a matter of debate but I can promise that you will *feel* healthier and that alone is a big score in its favour.

Travellers in Lapland soon begin to wonder if words like 'remote' or 'isolated' are really strong enough to convey the feeling of moving about in an unspoilt region so vast that any concept of a beginning or end to its limits is almost meaningless. Swedish Lapland covers nearly 100,000 square miles, which is getting on for a quarter of the entire country but fewer people live here than in an average-size provincial town. The terrain is mountains, forest and lakes with the mountains lower and more rounded to the south. One seventh of the region lies above the Arctic Circle.

While the Lappish race numbers about 35,000, only 10,000 of them are in Sweden. The rest inhabit some part of the north polar region which stretches from Norway across to Finland and Russia. They have their own language (but also speak Swedish), their own culture, and their own representatives to fight for their rights. They are a nomadic people but wandering has not made them less conscious of their traditions and history, which can be traced back to the time of the Romans. Among their contributions to Scandinavian civilization is the use of skis as an effective means of transport. The word 'ski' derives from Skridfinrna, the old Scandinavian name for Lapland, skrid or skrida meaning to slide.

The Lapps' tradition means of livelihood are hunting, fishing and reindeer-breeding, all highly skilled tasks but the latter a minority occupation also involving the hazards of keeping control of a herd when it embarks on its winter migration from the mountains to below the tree line where pasture can more easily be nuzzled out from beneath the snow. Reindeer meat is nowadays popular in Sweden (though it used to be regarded as a low-grade food) and there is even some export to Denmark and Germany but the herds are no longer an exclusive means of earning a living.

It could not be otherwise since the Lapps no longer make their everyday clothes from reindeer hide, or live in the traditional wigwam-shaped homes, which consisted of

16 A round-up of a Lappish reindeer herd.

reindeer skins draped round a simple scaffolding, or use reindeer for their fetching and carrying. The irony is that the reindeer has lost its central place in the Lapp economy just at a time when extensive rights and privileges have been extended to the nomadic Lapps to help them maintain the herds. They have a monopoly of reindeer breeding, free access to vast grazing areas and the freedom to hunt and fish anywhere in their region. At present there are about a quarter of a million reindeer in Sweden.

But other sources of income are opening up, not least the tourist industry with its ever-lengthening queue of nature seekers who regard the Lappish community with the fascination of intrepid explorers discovering the lost city. The Lapps are mildly tolerant of the invasion from the south and are happy to sell their superb craft products and even to wear their national dress for the sake of the photographers. But they do draw the line at having uninvited guests dropping in for a look round their homes, an experience which is not entirely unheard of and, more commonly, they sharply resent being asked how many reindeer they own, a question which is about as ill-mannered as asking your host how much money he has in the bank.

Some Lapps are directly involved in the tourist business – as shopkeepers or guides. Others profit from the tourists by selling the products of Lappish handicraft. These can be bought all over Sweden, but the best way to capture an impression of the range of Lappish domestic industry is to visit Jokkmokk, a community near the centre of the region where there is a conglomeration of craftsmen and artists. The leading Lappish painter, Lars Pirak, lives at Jokkmokk, also Ellen Kitok-Andersson whose original contribution to handicraft technique is making baskets and bowls from the roots of pine and other trees. Ornaments carved from reindeer horn are immensely popular with those who look for distinctively individualistic items of decoration. But even among these exclusively fashioned souvenirs there is nothing quite so unexpected as the Lappish style of embroidery. The art is performed, not with ordinary cotton, but with pewter, which by a lengthy process of rolling, shaping and winding is converted into a slender thread. The Lapps use it to adorn straps and belts and colourful heavy flannel clothing.

The time for buying in Jokkmokk is in the winter when they hold their annual fair, an event which originated with an understandable desire to lift the depression of the dark months. Nowadays there are charter tours from Denmark and Germany and an influx of Swedish visitors from the south, all keen to buy home-knitted woollies, fur hats and gloves and – this year perhaps – something more exclusive to show off at home. But there can be no hope of finding bargain prices. There is too much money chasing too few goods for that. At a recent Jokkmokk fair a Dane paid £700 for a bear skin and even after parting with his cash remained convinced of the wisdom of his purchase. A pine root basket from Ellen Kitok-Andersson can cost anything up to £200, though, she hastens to explain that a single item may require her to put in two months' full-time work. The roots must be collected, peeled and cleaned before the arduous task of weaving can even begin. With visitors paying out so much for a memento of their trip it might be thought unreasonable to worry greatly about the cost of accommodation. But here as almost everywhere else in Sweden there is the cheap option of looking after yourself in a rented cabin. The consolation of economy-style subsistence, is being able to save enough for an occasional visit to the Engelmarkska Hotel where they serve delicious reindeer steak with fresh cloudberries and cream to follow.

Even though the Lapps have the strongest regard for what can only be described as a primitive culture, they have not remained entirely isolated from the technological society. Kiruna, the great mining town, produces some twenty million tons of high-grade iron ore each year. The measure of this enterprise can be judged by the certain knowledge that at present capacity reserves are sufficient for an indefinite period of operation. Kiruna is further north than any other city in

Sweden, but in terms of land surface it is also the largest, not only in Sweden but in the world. It must be admitted that most of this area of 550 square miles in uninhabited and that the population is no more than 30,000; still the local people skip round that by proudly diverting your attention to the fact that within their city limits is Kebnekajse, one of the highest mountains in Scandinavia, and if that does not impress you where else can you see the midnight sun from your own back door?

A short drive from Kiruna is Nikkaluokta, which is only worth mentioning because it is the coldest place in Sweden. Among the few crazy enough to live there is a famous amateur weatherman known as the King of Kebnekajse. His forecasts, popularly acknowledged to be uncannily accurate, are based on his observations of plant growth and the eating habits of reindeer and fish. But for his own area he need only look out of the window to predict 'snow in high places'.

The Lapps are not entirely happy about Kiruna. They see huge wealth being created in a country which they regard as their own and they ask why is it so little of the reward finds it way to the local people. The complaint is echoed by many Swedes who believe that the prosperous and booming south uses the rest of the country in much the same way as industrialised nations once exploited their colonies – as ill-paid providers of national resources. One of the depressing sights in the north is the number of abandoned pulp mills, especially in Ångermanland province. Timber is still the major industry but the manufacturing processes have been moved to the south.

The problem was acknowledged by the national government when the north, or two-thirds of the country with less than twenty per cent of the total population and nearly fifty per cent of the unemployed, was declared a development area eligible for industrial grants. The conditions for these handouts have been the subject of intense debate but as a general rule a business must show promise of being able to survive independently to be eligible for aid. This begs the question, of course, as to how long a particular industry needs to establish itself in what in many ways is an unfavourable commercial environment. The idea of following a direct grant with operating subsidies may offend the rules of sound finance as practised by the Treasury but unless the principle is conceded it is unlikely that the growth economy will spread very far north. The biggest test case will be Steelworks 80, the biggest single industrial investment ever undertaken by the Swedish government. Steelworks 80, which is being built at Lulea, will employ some 2,500 workers when it opens in 1980, and indirectly provide jobs for a further 11,000. As a measure of the scale of problems involved in this enterprise, it was recently conceded that one or two icebreakers would be needed to guarantee round the year shipping of steel products.

To supplement the investment in factories and equipment, a manpower training and retraining programme is financed by the government, and as part of the revival of mainstream cultural activity, the latest of Sweden's universities has been set up at Umeå. This town which has grown rapidly in the fifteen years since the university accepted its first students, has attracted several more cultural institutions and stimulated others to take on new life. One such in the second category is Västerbottens Museum, the premier centre for research into all matters relating to the social history of the North.

Almost everyone who travels to the north by road soon has a fair impression of the economic advances so far made in the underdeveloped regions. Nearly all the new job opportunities are concentrated on the east side following the line of the coast and the best motor route, the E4. From Uppsala, the road crosses flat farming country to the sea at Gävle and then hugs the coast as it advances up through Söderham, Hudiksvall, Sundsvall, Härnösand, Örnsköldsvik, Umeå, Skellefteå, Piteå (known as the Riviera of the North because it has good weather throughout the summer) and Luleå, also popular with tourists, especially those who like the idea of boating in and about an archipelago of 300 islands. A few miles west of Luleå at Boden, is the northernmost golf course in the world.

Going on from Luleå the coast road touches only one more town of any size, Haparanda, before crossing the Finish border.

The E4 is a favoured route among tourists who have a good choice of stopping-off points and of diversionary inland trips. The latest and in many ways the most appealing of the motorway connections is the Blå Vägen, or Blue Road, so named because it follows a chain of lakes and rivers across the country from Umeå to the Norwegian border. Looking in the opposite direction for opportunities to vary the scenery, there are regular ferry services to Finland starting from Sundsvall, Örnsköldsvik and Umeå. Swedish holidaymakers from the south frequently choose to make the return journey through one or other of the neighbouring countries, a reminder, if one is needed, that after traversing Sweden the exploration of Scandinavia has only just began.

Postscript

It may be a little late to make an issue of it, but I should emphasise that this book is one man's view of Sweden. I make no claim to providing a comprehensive guide to all the attractions of the country. There are places, people and events I have missed either because I do not happen to think they are very important (but some will undoubtedly argue to the contrary) or because I have not been able to bring them into range of my travelling experience. But my conscience is clear. Impressions of Sweden, boldly drawn images of the people and their environment, are rare. Yet is seems to me that something of this sort is essential for anyone visiting the country for the first time. What is needed is a broad context of information into which relevant detailed factual knowledge can be slotted. For if there is one basic truth to be stated about Sweden, it is that facts are for free. Help and advice on what to see and how to see it are readily available, in all major European languages, at all tourist centres.

Index